# Using t
# suppor
# learning

**DENISE E MURRAY**
**PAM MCPHERSON**

A M E P
RESEARCH CENTRE

SERIES EDITOR DENISE E MURRAY
TEACHING WITH NEW TECHNOLOGY SERIES

Published by the
National Centre for English Language Teaching and Research
Macquarie University, Sydney NSW 2109
for the AMEP Research Centre on behalf of the
Department of Immigration and Multicultural and Indigenous Affairs

McPherson, Pam, 1946– .

Using the Web to support language learning.

Bibliography.

ISBN 1 74138 102 9.

1. English language - Study and teaching. 2. Educational technology. 3. World Wide Web.
4. Internet in education. I. Murray, Denise E. II. National Centre for English Language
Teaching and Research (Australia). III. Title. (Series: Teaching with new technology series).

407.1

**MACQUARIE**
UNIVERSITY ~SYDNEY

The AMEP Research Centre is a consortium of the National Centre for English Language
Teaching and Research (NCELTR) at Macquarie University in Sydney, and the School of
Educational Studies at La Trobe University in Melbourne. The Research Centre was
established in January 2000 and is funded by the Commonwealth Department of
Immigration and Multicultural and Indigenous Affairs.

Project Manager: Louise Melov
Production Supervisor: Kris Clarke
Design and DTP: Helen Lavery
Cover design: Helen Lavery
Printed by: Ligare Pty Ltd

# Contents

# Acknowledgments

This book reports on research conducted collaboratively by Adult Migrant English Program (AMEP) teachers and the authors as part of the Special Project Research Program at the AMEP Research Centre, funded by the Department of Immigration, Multicultural and Indigenous Affairs, Canberra. The book frames this research within the broader research on using the Internet for communication in language teaching and learning.

Special thanks are due to the AMEP teachers who collaborated in these action research projects. Also, we thank the AMEP service providers who encouraged participation of their teachers and the curriculum coordinators who helped organise professional development sessions and made it possible for teachers to be released from their classes.

The teachers whose work is referred to here are:

**acl Pty Ltd, Sydney**

| | |
|---|---|
| Ali Baharlou | Peter Norton |
| Najia Haimd | Cathy Tun |
| Sarah Houston | Hale Unat |
| Stephen Mansfield | |

**Qld TAFE Language and Literacy Services**

| | |
|---|---|
| Bojan Blatnik | Philippa Lipscomb |
| Steven Endres | Sven Puetter |
| Norma King Koi | |

**West Coast College of TAFE** (Perth, Western Australia)

Nita Johnson

# Series introduction

*Teaching with New Technology* is a series that provides teachers with practical, research-based approaches to using computer-based technologies in their language classrooms.

We have deliberately chosen to use the term 'computer-based technologies' to highlight the technologies where the computer is an obvious tool. Many other classroom tools and artefacts use digital technology, but they do not involve computers as machines in any obvious way. Such tools and artefacts include VCRs, mobile phones, clocks and language labs. These new computer-based technologies were initially taken up by teachers who had a passion for computer technology. Now that these technologies have been used in language education for almost two decades, many other teachers want to explore their use in their own classrooms. Language teachers are interested in using computer-based technologies both to facilitate language learning and to help their learners acquire the new literacies of the digital age (see, for example, Snyder 2002). In English language education in particular, teachers of migrants and refugees realise they need to help their learners acquire computer skills since students are likely to take jobs that require familiarity with a range of digital literacies. In many countries where English is being learned as the global language for wider communication, students want to learn English to access the new technologies. While still only 10 per cent of the world population is online, digital literacies are increasingly becoming an essential tool for social, educational and occupational worlds.

The goal of this series is to provide teachers who are new to using computer-based technologies in language teaching with practical techniques and lessons they can use in their classrooms. There is an assumption that teachers are familiar with the Web in other aspects of their lives and that they are experienced language teachers.

> *[I]t is not so much the computer but the kinds of tasks and activities that learners do on the computer that can make the difference …*
>
> (Hoven 1999: 149)

The philosophy behind the series is that, as language teaching professionals, teachers want more than hints and techniques; rather, professional teachers want to understand the research and theory on which teaching approaches are built. They are also interested in understanding which issues surrounding the use of computer-based technologies still need to be explored and in conducting research in their own classrooms. While this series focuses on the adult learner, many of the activities can be used in classrooms of children and young adults.

Although the various features of the new technologies often overlap in use inside and outside the classroom, teachers (and learners) need to be able to approach teaching (and learning) with these new technologies in incremental stages. Therefore, each book in the series focuses primarily on one aspect of using computer-based technologies in the language classroom.

Each book:

- summarises the principal findings about the use of computer-based technologies to support teaching and learning in language programs. This section includes specific research from the AMEP action research projects of teachers we worked with over two states. It also includes relevant research reported elsewhere.
- offers practical suggestions for teaching using these technologies. These suggestions are provided to help teachers who have not used the new technologies very often (or at all) in teaching. Some suggestions include a series of steps; others provide an idea that could be incorporated in a lesson.
- provides general lesson plans for some suggestions. These lesson plans are indicative, rather than prescriptive so that teachers working in a variety of contexts with learners from a variety of different language levels might find them useful.
- raises issues that teachers can explore in their own classrooms.

Many of the suggestions for teachers to explore involve action research, a research methodology for practitioners to investigate their own work practices. In educational settings, action research provides teachers with a tool for:

- planning what and how they will investigate;
- teaching based on what they want to investigate;

- observing their practice; and
- reflecting on their observations.

This process is then repeated, with teachers changing their practice based on their observations and reflections, and then beginning the cycle again (see, for example, Kemmis and McTaggart 1988; Burns 1995). An extensive bibliography is provided for teachers who want to explore any of the concepts and findings discussed in this series. The bibliography, which includes both referenced materials and materials for further reading, is organised by chapter at the end of each book.

# Introduction

The chapters in this volume are organised around a variety of different ways learners can use the World Wide Web to achieve their language, content and Web learning goals. This does not mean, however, that technology should be driving the curriculum. Our assumption is that teachers will first decide on their objectives and then choose Web resources that facilitate student learning of those goals, where appropriate. While some of the activities are necessarily technical in nature, the teaching suggestions and lesson plans are situated in language learning. The perspective we take in this volume is that Web-based activities should have a technical skill teaching purpose, a pedagogical reason (for example, distance learning) or a language learning purpose – or all three.

We have included the Web strategies and activities most commonly used by language teachers and structured the chapters around those different uses, while recognising that we are using a linear organisation for a non-linear, interconnected phenomenon. This linear organisation, however, will help teachers find teaching activities and tasks easily.

## Participating in a digital world

For language learners to participate in an increasingly digital world, they will need to use the technology via English to meet their social, personal and educational needs. To do this, they need to learn to navigate the Web, using it to find information and often to provide information. Many of the learners in our studies were unfamiliar with computers and being online, and they needed scaffolded instruction on how to acquire the skills and literacies of this new digital world. To access information on the Web, learners need to be online, that is, using a computer that is connected to the Internet. The Internet is the worldwide network of computer networks that connects computer users who gain access through an ISP (Internet Service Provider), which may be provided through school or work or for which learners can sign up in the same way as for a telephone service. The World Wide Web, on the other hand, is a hypertext-based system for accessing a variety of resources on the Internet. It is possible to navigate the Web at work, school, library or Internet cafe without having a personal Internet account. However, since research has shown that using computer-mediated communication (CMC) can facilitate language learning (see *Communicating on the Net*, a volume in this series), we will include teaching suggestions and lesson plans that combine using CMC and information from the Web. CMC skills that learners need include communicating through chat, email and discussion lists, and also being able to send and manage information via CMC such as address books or sending and receiving attachments.

To frame our discussions, we will first summarise some of the findings about teaching and learning using the Web: the advantages and disadvantages of the authentic language on the Web, the importance of scaffolding learning, and the literacies learners need to use the Web for language learning.

## Authentic language input

Second language learning research has discussed the importance of authentic materials and tasks in language learning. Little, Devitt and Singleton (1994), for example, have shown that learners find authentic texts more motivating than pedagogical texts. Others (for example, Bachman and Palmer 1996) have noted that communicative language ability is situation-specific and that therefore pedagogical tasks should mirror as much as possible tasks learners will engage in outside the classroom.

> *Letting English language learners onto the Internet is like dropping them in an ocean of words, concepts, genres, tenses, even other languages.*
>
> (Mansfield 2002: 3)

The Web has potential for both types of authenticity. It provides learners with unlimited opportunities for accessing authentic language; however, this very access may be a disadvantage. Learners may find a site with language beyond their current linguistic competence, or they may find sites that use inappropriate language or culture for the particular learners (for example, pornographic sites), or they may come to rely on the Internet for accurate information, but use information from a site written by schoolchildren or a site that uses propaganda or a site with advertising dressed up as information. While webpages designed by schoolchildren may be interesting and may even be accurate, they may not be. Many personal sites or sites selling a particular product or idea may present biased or incorrect information. It is therefore necessary for learners to learn the skills for and practise evaluating websites.

Additionally, since the Web is now an essential part of the fabric of work, personal life and education in many countries, using the Web to find information for classroom tasks mirrors what many learners will need to do in their lives. However, for learners to be able to apply their classroom learning outside the classroom, teachers will need to design tasks that are in fact similar to those outside the classroom.

## Scaffolding learning

Because of the vastness of the Web, teachers need to carefully scaffold tasks and activities. 'Scaffolding refers to support that is designed to provide the assistance necessary to enable learners to accomplish tasks and develop understandings that they would not quite be able to manage on their own' (Hammond 2001: 3). While scaffolding has been used to refer to both planned or designed-in instruction and in situ or contingent instruction (see, for example, Hammond 2001), here we are primarily referring to the scaffolding teachers build into their lesson plans and activities. To scaffold searching for information on the Web, teachers need to consider the language, content, navigation and design of webpages. Some teachers (for example, Mansfield 2002) have developed a series of structured activities that have helped learners acquire the skills to search and navigate the Web by themselves. Others (for example King Koi 2002) have structured learning by choosing websites and categorising them using a learning management system. Yet another teacher (Puetter 2002) has designed his own website for learners to use, while others (for example, Blatnik 2002; Unat 2002) have chosen only ESL sites where learners can learn the language through structured activities. Teachers also need strategies for determining appropriate sites – in terms of language, content and Web design (see Chapters One and Four).

## Learning new literacies

While the Web contains texts that follow the conventions of print-based texts (for example, narratives, information texts), the Web also contains new configurations of texts, where more than one genre might appear on one webpage, for example. In addition, not all Web literacy is text-based; indeed, visual literacy

*The Internet is a virtual minefield. In order to negotiate this minefield (or at least reduce casualties), classes need to be well thought through and websites (where possible) chosen discerningly.*
(Norton 2002: 7)

(see, for example, Kress 1997; Snyder 1999, 2002) can be found alongside text and may even be supplanting it. Familiar genres may develop new features, while new genres may appear. Additionally, the Web provides a hypertextual environment, rather than a linear one, presenting yet another literacy for learners to acquire (Tindale in press). Therefore, literacy skills learners may have acquired to read critically and write print text may not suffice when learners encounter the Web (Lipscomb 2002). Not only do our learners need the technical skills of computer literacy, but they also

*The Web invites a nonlinear, nonsequential, interactive medium for students, and reading skills must incorporate strategies to deal with multimedia and visual elements.*
(Sutherland-Smith 2002: 64)

need the language and literacies the new technologies require. Being literate in this technological era means making sense of varying combinations of text, signs, symbols, pictures and even sounds and moving pictures. And, making sense of it requires searching for

multimodal information and evaluating, interpreting and synthesising it. This book will help teachers and learners achieve the goal of becoming information literate in this information rich world.

Some useful general principles when using the Web in language teaching are (Robb, T 2004, personal communication, 23 November):

- Students working on computers are 'functionally deaf'; they are often mesmerised by the flickering screen. Devise some method to ensure students are paying full attention when you address the entire class. For example, students can be asked to turn off their monitors, turn their chairs away from the computer or put away their keyboards.

- Explicitly teach students how to bookmark sites that they may want to go back to later and how to categorise their bookmarks into useful groupings.

- Explicitly teach students how to copy and paste an URL into a document so they can readily keep the source of the information with the online text they have copied and saved.

## CHAPTER ONE

# Finding and selecting information on the Web

As learners develop their ability to find and select information on the Web, they will learn to integrate a variety of critical literacy skills – skimming, scanning, discriminating and categorising. When learners learn how to find and select information on the Web, they will be able to:

* identify words or concepts on a given topic;
* use search engines to find items based on words or phrases;
* use Web directories to find items based on topics or themes; and
* select appropriate and relevant information from a Web search.

'Surfing the net' is a term in current usage. However, such an unstructured approach to finding information on the Web is unlikely to result in finding useful information and often results in frustration. Consequently, Internet companies have developed two different ways to find information: search engines and directories, each of which requires different skills and uses a different approach.

Search engines such as *Google* or *Yahoo!* are based on words or phrases while directories are based on topics and themes. This difference is blurring somewhat as *Google* and *Yahoo!* also have a directory and *Yahoo!* actually uses *Google* as its search engine. Most search engines rank the results by popularity or relevance; *Google* ranks by both popularity and relevance. The teachers we worked with found that their learners found *Google* and *Yahoo!* the simplest search engines to use.

*Single words often presented the surfing student with hundreds of pages of material which was too time consuming to sort out and get to the required information.*
(Baharlou 2002: 5)

To use a search engine effectively, learners need to know exactly the word or phrase on which to base their search. One teacher in our studies (Mansfield 2002), having elicited from students what they wanted to write a report on (Australian animals), had students search for 'animals', only to find that the search resulted in a long list of pornographic sites. He then suggested they use actual species names (for example, koala, kangaroo), only to find a list of (mostly) companies that had named themselves after Australian animals. He finally found that a search for 'Australian animals' produced a list of appropriate sites. It is therefore wise for teachers to preview the search results of any search engine and search words they plan to use to avoid accidentally displaying inappropriate material.

Directories such as *Yahoo!* were designed to bring some order to the chaos and plethora of websites. They are designed around categories and sub-categories. While these may be easier to navigate, they require the learner to categorise the topic they are looking for. So, if learners were looking for Australian animals, they could categorise this topic either under animals or under travel (Australia). Since the categories have been predetermined by the company, the learner needs to understand what subcategories might appear as part of the higher level categories, which in itself can be a useful language learning activity.

Once learners have conducted a search, they need to be able to scan the list of search results and select a website that might have the information they need. Teachers have found that learners need to be able to identify sites written by children that may or may not have accurate

*If a student is searching for factual data, an official site like a government site is often the first one they may want to check. While their search shouldn't stop here, it is always a good place to start.*

(Mansfield 2002: 4)

information; or sites that are primarily advertising tools. Teachers have suggested strategies such as scanning all the options before choosing, choosing on the basis of the URL, or conducting another search, but with more specific words (see, for example, Mansfield 2002).

Once learners have selected a site, they still need selection skills. Again, teachers have found a number of strategies that assist learners: avoiding sites with difficult language; avoiding sites that are primarily selling; scanning for relevant keywords and vocabulary; skimming for overall gist; and, recognising relevant genres (see Chapter Four for more specific research on this issue). Once at a site, learners encounter another method for finding information – links. Again, they need to use critical thinking and selection skills in deciding which links might be productive and on the topic.

As well as learning the reading skills of skimming and scanning and the generic skills of critical thinking, problem solving and evaluating information, students

*Effective searching of the Web is a complex reasoning and decision-making process.*
(Todd 2000:119)

also learn technology skills needed for the workplace and engage in experiences in contexts similar to those in which technology is used outside the classroom (Ginsberg 1998). Teachers have also noted that pre-teaching offline how to search the Web can also be used to assess (and teach) other aspects of language such as how to respond to complex spoken instructions or read a procedural text.

# Teaching suggestions

## Not using email, chat or other CMC

- Demonstrate in class the procedures for finding a search engine page and typing in a search word.
- Have students list topics of interest and then subtopics within each topic.
- Divide the class into two teams. Have each team think of a topic and then five subtopics within it. Have teams give each other the super-ordinate topic. Have each team guess the subtopics the other team chose.
- Have students choose a topic. Write it on the whiteboard and then ask students to think of as many subtopics as they can. Write or have the students write these subtopics as a mind map. Ask students to think about what subtopics might appear that are not relevant to their topic and that they would therefore want to eliminate.
- Have students choose a topic and determine at least three aspects of the topic that they want to find out about on the Web. Have students write the topic and its aspects as Boolean functions (that is, using the operators *and*, *not*, and *or*).
- Print out the results of a Web search. Have each student choose a different site to investigate. Have students find their site and report back to the class on its usefulness. (Provide a list of criteria for evaluating sites. A useful set of criteria can be found at http://www.scu.edu.au/library/tgcc/guides/websiteeval.pdf)
- Have students use a directory to find websites on a specified topic. Have students use a search engine to find websites on the same topic. In class, have students compare the findings – do the same websites appear in each search method? Conduct a class discussion about the reasons why the results might be different.
- Have students read the URL of the results of a search engine and identify the different domains (*edu*, *gov*, *mil*, *com*, *net* and ~ for personal webpages). Discuss with students which they think would be most reliable and why.
- Divide the class into three teams. Provide a general topic and specific information students are to find about that topic. Have each team use

a different search engine (for example, *Google, Yahoo!, Ask Jeeves, Web Wombat, AltaVista, Excite, MSN Search*) to find the specific information. Have the whole class evaluate the information found and discuss what criteria each search engine seems to be using. Discuss which would be the most useful criteria for their search.

- Divide the class into four teams. Provide a general topic and specific information students are to find about that topic. Have each team use a different search engine. Have two use world-wide search engines and two use Australia-specific search engines (for example, *Google Australia, Yahoo! Australia & NZ, Web Wombat*) to find the specific information. Ask the whole class to compare and contrast the different lists of URL sites from each search.

- Divide the class into two teams. Provide a general topic and specific information students are to find about that topic. Have one team use a search engine and the other use a directory. Have the whole class evaluate the information found and the ease of the different search types.

- Have all students go to a specific website. Ask each student to choose one of the links on the site and go to that site. With the whole class, compare the different sites for relevance, level of language, accuracy of information and ease of reading.

- Demonstrate, using the data projector, how to move through a chain of links and how the browser shows ancestors (path to the current website).

- Demonstrate, using the data projector, how to move through a chain of links and how the site takes users outside the original site. Explain how to go back to the original site by retyping the URL or searching in the pull-down menu and how to read the history of the links to help them.

- Have students use a search engine to find websites about their town. Have students in groups choose different websites and find specific information about their town. Have students evaluate which site had relevant information and which was the most accurate. Have students categorise sites according to their readability, the reliability of the information and the age groups of the authors. Ask students how they decided their categories.

- Write a set of questions about a topic recently covered in class. Have students search the Web to find the answer to the questions. Make this activity a game, with a prize for the student who finds the most correct answers first.

## Using email, chat or other CMC

- Have each student use a search engine for a specified topic. Ask students to select an URL, go to the website and copy the URL and send it in an email to the class. Have students select two websites from those that have been sent to them, go to the website and evaluate the usefulness of the information. (Provide criteria for how to evaluate the appropriateness of the information.)

- Have each student use a search engine to find an e-greeting card site and then email a greeting card to friends and family.

- Ask students to use a directory to find an online version of a local newspaper and choose an article that would be of interest to friends and family in their home countries. Have students cut and paste the URL for this article and send it to friends and family in their home countries.

## Lesson plans

---

### Lesson not using email, chat or other CMC

**Objective:**  Students will be able to refine Web searches.

**Materials:**  Data projector, Internet-connected computers.

**Procedure:**

Search 1

- Have the class choose a topic on which to do a search on the Web (for example, events in their city, Australian animals, a current political event).
- Using a data projector, type the suggested topic into a well-known search engine and display the results of the search.
- Print out the first page of the results.
- Identify the types of information that are likely to be found on each of the websites with the class.

Search 2

- Have students refine the topic by narrowing it.
- Using a data projector, type the suggested refined topic into a well-known search engine and display the results of the search.
- Print out the first page of the results.
- Identify the types of information that are likely to be found on each of the websites with the class.

Search 3

- Have students refine the topic using Boolean operators.
- Using a data projector, type the suggested refined topic into a well-known search engine and display the results of the search.
- Print out the first page of the results.
- Identify the types of information that are likely to be found on each of the websites with the class.
- Compare and contrast the websites from the three different searches with the whole class.

**Extension:**

- Have students in groups select a topic, refine it and then conduct a search.
- Have groups report their findings to the class.

## Lesson not using email, chat or other CMC

**Objective:** Students will be able to find websites specifically designed to help learners of English.

**Materials:** Data projector, Internet-connected computers.

**Procedure:**

- Have students brainstorm words they think they will find on an ESL/EFL website.
- Using a data projector, type each suggestion into a well-known search engine and display the results of the search.
- Compare and contrast the results of each search with the whole class.
- Have students choose websites from these searches to visit.
- Using the data projector, display the homepages of these websites.
- Ask students whether they think each website is in fact a language teaching website. Have them evaluate the usefulness of each website from viewing the homepage.

**Extension:**

- See Chapter Two for activities using ESL websites.

## Lesson not using email, chat or other CMC

**Objective:** Students will be able to evaluate the results of a Web search.

**Materials:** Data projector, Internet-connected computers.

**Procedure:**

- Have the class choose a topic of interest.
- Use a well-known search engine to carry out a search on the topic. Use the data projector to display the search.
- With students, evaluate each entry on the first page of the search results. Develop criteria for evaluating Web search results and predicting useful sites, such as relevance, commercial sites versus government and educational sites, and level of language.
- Choose one of the websites. Go to that website and evaluate the information in terms of whether it meets the class predictions of its usefulness.
- Have students brainstorm subtopics within that topic and choose one of the subtopics.
- Divide the class into groups of five and have them carry out a search on the subtopic. Ask each group to choose a website they think will be the most useful from the first page of results and then evaluate it.
- Have groups report back to the class as to which website they chose and why and whether their predictions held.
- Based on the whole class and group activities, jointly develop criteria for choosing useful and appropriate websites from search engine results.
- Discuss the advantages and disadvantages of choosing a narrow topic (the subtopic above) or a broader topic (the original topic above).

**Extension:**

- Have each group summarise the information they found on the subtopic and topic.

## Lesson using email, chat or other CMC

**Objective:** Students will be able to collaborate on a project in which they retrieve information from the Web, write a report and share information.

**Materials:** Internet-connected computers.

**Procedure:**

- Divide the class into groups and have each group choose a topic for their project, for example, movies, Australian animals, restaurants, a country.
- Have each student choose one aspect of the topic, for example, a particular movie, Australian animal, restaurant or city, and do a search on the Web for a photo and information on that aspect.
- Ask each student to copy the photo and write a report on their particular aspect of the topic.
- Have each student email the photo and report to the other members of the group.
- Ask the students to meet in their groups and decide how to present their project to the class, using a presentation program.
- Have groups present their projects to the class.

**Extension:**

- Organise students to post their presentation on the class website.

**Note:** Sending email attachments is taught in *Communicating on the Net*, a volume in this series.

# Issues to explore

## Issue  Teaching offline

Do students benefit from having particular skills demonstrated offline?

### Exploration – action research

#### Using an overhead projector to demonstrate using a search engine

- Using an overhead projector and printouts, demonstrate how to use a search engine and how to select a website from the search results.
- Have students search the Web and choose one appropriate site.
- Observe and take notes on whether students can do the task easily, what questions they ask and what problems they have.

#### Using a data projector to demonstrate using a directory

- Using a data projector, demonstrate how to use a directory and how to select a website from the search result.
- Have students search the Web and choose one appropriate site.
- Observe and take notes on whether students can do the task easily, what questions they ask and what problems they have.
- Decide which demonstration medium is most effective for your learners – overhead or data projector.

## Issue  Scaffolding learning

Which is the most appropriate teaching/learning approach for learners to acquire the skills for retrieving information from the Web – explicit teaching, scaffolded instruction or discovery learning?

### Exploration – questions to think about

- Think about your particular learners. How familiar are they with searching the Web? Are those that are unfamiliar anxious about using the Web? What is the cause of this anxiety? How do they adjust their goals to minimise anxiety?
- Think about learners in an entirely different context from yours (for example, young learners/older learners; ESL/EFL; conversation class/academic English class). How might they respond to scaffolded instruction or to discovery learning?

CHAPTER TWO

# Using ESL websites

Many ESL websites offer teaching materials, lessons plans, games and other instructional resources that are freely available to students and teachers. They continue a long-standing practice of sharing and collaboration among TESOL teachers. Now through the Internet, this sharing extends world-wide and reaches out directly to students. A large number of these websites have been created by ESL teachers and along with instructional materials for students, they offer teachers opportunities for professional development by inviting contributions, ideas and discussion from teachers around the globe. An example is *The Internet TESL Journal* where ESL/EFL teachers all over the world contribute to the self-study quizzes for ESL/EFL students. (See http://iteslj.org/)

These ESL websites provide a valuable online service for teachers and learners alike. Teachers can find prepared lessons and materials addressing English language development in diverse content areas, curriculum and academic disciplines. Students of all ages, interests and learning goals can independently choose online instructional materials and activities that meet their specific language learning needs, and access them in their own time and at their own pace.

Jones (2000) in Moote (2002) examines the characteristics of some online learning materials for students and describes three models of online learning sites for students: distributive, tutorial and cooperative.

In the **distributive** model, materials or lesson sheets are available for learners to study independently. Students respond to reading or listening passages by completing multiple-choice, gap-filling or other exercises. The software allows students to get immediate feedback on their answers.

The **tutorial** model is often found on fee-for-service websites that offer two-way communication between the teacher and the learner using email, chat, telephone or video conferencing.

The **cooperative** model allows students in the course to communicate with each other as well as with the teacher.

Ho Mei Lin (1997) advises teachers to evaluate online ESL materials carefully before assigning them for independent study. She reminds us that learning activities which only engage students in achieving scores

*There is a need to consider if the online resources teach students grammar items or merely test them.*

(Ho Mei Lin 1997)

on tests and quizzes do not necessarily help develop their proficiency or ability to use the language effectively and appropriately.

She recommends that teachers 'select self-directed tasks and programs that teach students how to work independently' (1997: 3) rather than direct them to a series of mindless drills or limit the choices they can make. It is crucial to provide feedback to the student, to offer choice of activity and to let them have ownership of their independent learning program.

*With a diverse range of links, the students are directed to different sites to suit their level of language and computer skills. For example, a word search puzzle, game or grammar task can be done at all levels. Students often choose their own activities and work at their own pace so no one has time constraints or feels threatened.*

(King Koi 2002)

King Koi's (2002) approach to using ESL websites with her students in an adult community education class draws on Jones's three models. She creates a class website that is password-protected and only accessible by her students.

She constructs a page of carefully researched links that includes ESL websites offering skills development in grammar, speaking, listening, reading, writing, spelling, pronunciation, general games and puzzles (**distributive**). These links are regularly updated and reviewed to keep pace with student learning. She begins each day with a lesson (**tutorial**) and assigns Web-based learning tasks to the class, many of which require interaction among the students (**cooperative**). While these tasks are in progress she monitors each student, giving individualised support where needed. Later, students choose independent learning activities and at the end of the session complete an evaluation sheet outlining what they have learned from each site.

Unat (2002) uses a range of ESL websites with elementary level adult students. She notes that the interactive instructions on ESL websites pose some difficulties for her students and prevent them from accessing the learning materials. After teaching them the structure of an ESL website, the functionality of hypertext links, drop-down lists and drag-and-drop buttons and the language accompanying these functions, students are able to locate and complete online learning activities independently on ESL sites.

*What I experienced was that because they [students] were unclear about the instructions most of them were unable to use their time effectively to do the activities.*

(Unat 2002)

The Web has opened up a wealth of language learning resources for ESL/EFL students. ESL websites have general and special interest collections that are adequate for most students' needs. By taking the time to select websites and activities carefully and by monitoring their students' progress, teachers can offer a good online learning experience and provide their students with skills to continue their language learning independently, in their own time and at their own pace.

# Teaching suggestions

## Requiring students to have computer skills

- When planning your course and assembling teaching materials, search the Web widely for ESL websites and learning activities that address the language skills you plan to teach. Over a number of courses you will develop a substantial list that can be categorised by language level, function or elements.

- Teach browser functions like *back, forward* and *stop* and ensure students have developed the mouse skills required for interactive activities found on ESL websites.

- Give explicit instruction on how to interact with learning activities so students become familiar with selecting from drop-down lists, responding to true/false questionnaires and using their mouse well for drag-and-drop responses.

- For students at beginner language levels or new to the Internet, offer a structured guide to the generic features of ESL sites and ensure they understand what is available on the site, and how to select preferred activities using links, buttons and other navigational devices.

- Beginners may need to learn the language of instructions commonly used on ESL websites. Teach the meanings of phrases like *click on, select, choose, go to* and allow a lot of structured practice before you expect them to work independently.

- Scan websites to choose those that meet your students' learning needs and then collate them on a class webpage of links. To accommodate the disparate learner levels in your class, categorise them by difficulty level.

- On your class webpage, categorise links in ways that help students find learning activities easily, for example, *pronunciation practice, listening to conversations, past tense quiz, making sentences, automotive wordsearch.*

- Encourage students to note the name and URL of sites they use and like so they can locate them independently.

- Create a monitoring system that allows you to check students' progress in using the ESL websites you select for them.

- Ask students to report quiz results, print out their responses, or evaluate the learning activities they have just completed. Ensure they or you keep a record of completed activities.

- In computer lab sessions, provide a range of different learning tasks, including teacher-led instruction, independent practice, extended learning and Web-based communication activities with you and classmates.
- Have regular reporting sessions where students take turns to introduce a favourite ESL website to the class, describe its best features and say why they like using it.
- As students become more confident and independent, encourage them to reflect on their learning needs, develop their own individualised learning plan and select a sequence of learning activities using ESL websites.

## Lesson plans

### Lesson requiring students to have computer skills

**Objective:** Students will learn to use interactive learning activities on ESL websites.

**Materials:** Class webpage, ESL websites, computer lab with Internet access.

**Procedure:**

- Prepare a class webpage with four to five links to ESL websites that use interactive functions, for example, *drop-down list, drag-and-drop, multiple-choice with feedback; true/false with feedback.*

- Ensure activity samples are within your students' linguistic range so they are not distracted by unfamiliar language.

- Using a data projector, click on a link to an ESL website's drop-down list.

- Point out the instructions to an activity and elicit from students the imperative used in the phrase, for example, *choose, select.* Elicit from students other synonyms that might be used.

- While you demonstrate, describe to students:
  - the mouse skill you use to select an item;
  - the next action you take to submit the response; and
  - how to use the browser *back* button to undo an action.

- Repeat the language and sequence of actions several times, inviting students to say the spoken instruction as you complete each action.

- Invite students to practise the same activity. They should follow the link to the same website activity, make a selection from the drop-down list, submit the response and then return to the list by using the back button.

- Assist individual students and invite pairs and groups to work together.

- Select a few students to demonstrate the procedure on your computer, using the language of instruction as they do so.

- Allow students free practice with the remaining two to three links on the class homepage and assist where necessary.

# Lesson requiring students to have computer and Internet skills

**Objective:** Students will use the class webpage to develop an individualised language learning program.

**Materials:** Class webpage and printout, ESL websites, individual evaluation form, computer lab.

**Procedure:**

Week 1

- Set up or revise your class homepage to ensure, for example, that all links are up to date and categorised in levels, that various language learning functions are listed and that you have included any other features of your choice.
- If your students need printouts, copy the webpage to a document, include check boxes for each item and print one for each student.
- Outline to your students the course goals, your approach to teaching these and examples of Web-based, print and classroom learning activities. Discuss the program with students, ensuring they understand which learning activities are mandatory, which are negotiable, and which can be done by individual choice.
- Demonstrate the links on the homepage, selecting samples at different levels and for different language learning functions.
- Hand out a simple needs analysis that invites students to choose individual priority learning areas within the framework of the course goals. Ensure that a manageable range of choices is offered.
- Ask students to select from the homepage the websites that may assist them in their priority learning areas.
- Ask students to prioritise some selected sites to use over the next week in free computer lab time, or for homework.

Week 2

- Ask students to form groups and discuss and evaluate their experience of the websites they used, and the extent to which they had supported or extended their learning.
- Ask students to complete an individual evaluation form of the previous week's learning through ESL websites.
- Ask students to review their first week's choices and choose links again for the second week's individual work.

## Lesson to use ESL websites to complete a task

**Objective:** Students will use ESL websites as a resource to support individual learning needs.

**Materials:** Class webpage and printout, ESL websites, individual evaluation form, Internet-connected computers.

**Procedure:**

- On your class homepage, provide a list of ESL resources and ESL websites that provide those resources, for example, thesaurus, dictionaries, grammar points, pronunciation.

- Divide the class into groups and allocate to each group the task of constructing one or more spoken or written texts, for example: application letter for a public service position, a set of possible job interview questions and responses, a short report on a recent work project, a resumé, a letter of complaint to a public authority.

- Have groups identify the subgroup of tasks to be done and allocate them among themselves based on the skills in their group.

- Make sure groups identify gaps in their knowledge, for example, what does a resumé look like?

- Have groups construct their texts, using ESL sites to find information and resources to assist them, and keeping records of the sites they used and their usefulness.

- Ask groups to report back to the class, demonstrating their completed text, listing information they acquired, the sources they used, and their evaluation of their usefulness.

# Issues to explore

### Issue  Using Web-based practice drills

Can ESL practice drills assist with language learning?

### Exploration – action research

- Assign a writing activity to a small group of students to establish their level of English.
- Assign Web-based practice drills to these students on the basis of the language learning needs demonstrated in the test activity.
- Monitor the amount of time students spend on each practice drill.
- At the end of the course or semester, assign the same writing activity and see what improvements the students have made.
- Interview the students about their attitudes to the practice drills and how they believe they assisted them.

### Issue  Selecting learning resources

Which learning resources on ESL websites do students prefer?

### Exploration – action research

- Prepare and administer a questionnaire asking students about their language learning needs and preferences for language learning materials and resources.
- Prepare a portal page with links to a number of ESL websites. Ensure students' preferences are included, but also add an equal number of other ESL websites and learning activities that you believe will be useful.
- Ask students to record the sites they used, the ones that were helpful and the most enjoyable to use. Include other questions of interest to you.
- At the end of the course, ask students to complete an individual evaluation form. In addition, conduct a group evaluation.
- Repeat this evaluation with a number of classes over a year or so. Look for patterns in the students' evaluations.

## CHAPTER THREE

# Listening online

'Teaching listening' has frequently been described as one of the more problematic areas of second language teaching and learning. Buck (1999) points out that the issues learners face in responding to spoken language are that:

- Speech is a set of acoustic signals and knowledge of the sound system of the language is needed to process the spoken text.
- Spoken language is different to written text. It is constructed differently, is more disjunctive and has 'disfluencies' like pauses, hesitations, self-corrections and repairs.
- Speech is fast and delivered in real time which means listeners need to process and respond quickly.

Although we may not precisely understand learners' experiences when they hear spoken English, studies in second language acquisition, psycholinguistics and the sociocultural aspects of spoken discourse offer some insights into the physiological aspects of hearing (Rost 2002), the psycholinguistic processing, and the dynamics of interaction between speaker and hearer (Chaudron, Loschky and Cook 1994; Rost 1994, 2002; Nunan and Miller 1995, 1997; Hoven 1999).

We now have a better understanding of the features of spoken texts and the teaching strategies that will help our students to understand and respond to spoken English in different situations (Ur 1984; Brown 1990; Nunan and Miller 1995; Burns 1997).

Teaching strategies can include those that focus on 'bottom-up' processing skills and 'top-down' processing skills. Using 'bottom-up' processing skills, students decode the sounds of English from small meaningful units or phonemes to whole stretches of discourse, as in a conversation, for example. Using 'top-down' processing, listeners draw on their own perceptions of the context or situation, their previous knowledge of the topic and their familiarity with the structure of the spoken text to 'reconstruct' what they hear from the speaker (Nunan 1997).

Until recently, limitations in Web technology prevented ESL website developers from offering the wide range of spoken texts and instructional activities that learners need to develop listening and comprehension skills.

Advances in Web technology and personal computing have led to a sudden and rapid increase in the number and range of online resources available to teachers and learners (Peterson 2001; Blatnik 2002; Cziko and Park 2003). Media players are now included in commercial software packages and are just as easily downloaded for free from the Internet. It is now almost standard practice for websites to include video and audio files on their sites including audio chat, and ESL websites in particular have been quick to capitalise on the opportunities for language learning that multimedia offers.

*[My] study results show that even very low-level students with no computer and language skills can benefit from suitable types of [Internet] listening resources.*
(Blatnik 2002)

The increasing range of online video and audio offers ESL students a multitude of opportunities to develop their understanding of spoken English. Teachers can increase students' exposure to spoken texts so that they hear spoken English more frequently; are exposed to more varieties of English and spoken texts; and can develop teaching programs tailored to their learners' individual needs and preferences.

*User-friendly computer technology empowers students to access vast numbers of extremely diverse online resources that can cater for the individual needs of students.*
(Blatnik 2002)

With these resources teachers can be highly selective about the kinds of texts they choose for learners. Teachers are now less reliant on unnaturally scripted stretches that misrepresent natural speech and don't prepare learners well for hearing the ways English is spoken in everyday life (Burns 1997). They can demonstrate the differences between spoken and written English more easily, choosing realistic

*L2 teachers will need to change their methods and lessons in order to allow and encourage their students to use the Internet to interact with native speakers of the language they are learning.*
Cziko and Park (2003)

representations of spoken discourse with natural features such as pause, hesitation and backtracking.

They can choose good models of spoken English using conversations, reports, interviews, and discussions in differing contexts, in a wide range of dialects, varieties and accents and with a variety of participants, allowing students to hear and identify the features of natural discourse in spoken English.

Students can access ESL listening sites that include different genres of spoken texts, and topics that include academic, vocational, and general interests such as the family, the arts, sports and music, and day-to-day activities such as shopping.

ESL sites offer audio and video texts for beginners that are shorter or delivered at a slower pace. Some provide transcripts and learners can read as they listen, replay as often as they like, and progress at their own pace. Advanced learners can choose audio or video on news sites with interviews and reports or discussions that exemplify natural features of authentic spoken discourse. In some cases, these sites also offer transcripts.

Ultimately, we can now provide learners with individual choice. We can design learning programs that respond to individual listening comprehension needs using a wide range of text styles and types, taking learner interests, needs and preferences into consideration (Burns 1997; Hoven 1999).

# Teaching suggestions

## Requiring students to have Web skills

- Decide what kind of listening texts and activities you want to include in your listening program before you search the Internet. It is easy to be distracted by the exciting range of resources, and a list of specific needs will speed up your search.
- Refer to your analysis of student needs when planning the kinds of spoken language texts your students should listen to. Decide if they need to hear news reports, lectures, interviews or casual conversations.
- List the interaction strategies your students are learning to use and need to hear demonstrated in the conversations they listen to.
- Identify specific or general interest topics that are most useful or interesting to your students.
- Prepare a rubric that includes types of spoken text, topics, language levels, learning activities and other criteria for choosing your online audio and video resources. This rubric will speed up your classification of resources and your search for materials when on the Web.
- In the classroom, teach the features of natural spoken texts. In this way, you can discuss issues about the context and register with students before they practise their listening skills online.
- In the classroom, teach listening strategies like listening for specific information and listening for gist so that learners understand their purpose and can apply them in online activities.
- Teach vocabulary related to the content before students listen to the text and encourage students to listen selectively for the vocabulary in some listening exercises.
- Have regular reporting back sessions in class where students evaluate their online experiences, and report on the usefulness of sites and materials and how they perceive the online learning experience.
- Have students report to the whole class on interesting topics, reports, dialogues or lectures they listened to online.

## Finding listening websites

- With your prepared list and rubric for choosing and evaluating resources, browse specialist ESL listening sites, general ESL sites, and non-educational sites in that order. Most ESL listening websites have extensive catalogues and links to their collections, making your research task easier, while many general ESL sites have audio collections as well.

- Access public broadcaster sites, like ABC and BBC. Many of these have excellent English language learning sites and the technical features of their audio and video files are generally more efficient and workable than non-expert sites.

- Create a class website that is a portal to online resources, categorised by genre, level of difficulty, or any other criteria that are useful to your class.

- Create a WebQuest (see also Chapter Six) that requires students to collect and collate information only available from audio/video sites.

- Use news, sports and other special interest sites to make the listening program interesting and motivational.

- Use websites that have both audio and written text to support both reading and listening skills.

- Develop individualised plans with sites, exercises and activities for students to complete. Ensure they report on learning achieved rather than sites visited.

- Create an online evaluation rubric so students can report on sites or tasks as they complete their exercises.

# Lesson plans

## Lesson requiring students to have Web skills

**Objective:** Students will become aware of the different varieties of spoken English used on websites.

**Materials:** List of media websites, comprehension questions, evaluation checklist, print-based articles, Internet-connected computers.

**Procedure:**

Beforehand

- Prepare a list of URLs from different countries for media websites that use audio, for example, CNN, Fox (USA); BBC (UK); ABC, ABC Asia Pacific (Australia).
- Prepare a list of questions students can use to show their understanding of audio news items.
- Prepare a checklist that students can use to evaluate the comprehensibility of audio items.

On the day

- Provide students with print-based newspaper and magazine articles about a current news topic.
- Review their understanding of the issues in the article and the language used to describe them.
- Discuss the perspectives of the writers and how they use language to convey them.
- Provide students with the list of news websites.
- Ask students to listen to online news from three different countries and respond to the listening comprehension tasks.
- Download transcripts of the audio so students can check their listening comprehension.
- Ask students to evaluate the sites according to how well they understood the news items.
- Discuss with students the different varieties, accents and language usage in the news items they have heard.
- Encourage students to read website forums on the news item topic and contribute an opinion of their own.

## Lesson requiring students to have Web skills

**Objective:** Teachers will manage disparate student needs.

**Materials:** Class webpage, Internet-connected computers.

**Procedure:**

Beforehand

- Prepare a list of websites that include ESL sites with good listening activities, as well as websites with 'authentic' audio and transcripts.
- Create a class webpage of links to the websites you have chosen.
- Classify the links in folders for advanced, beginner and intermediate learners.
- Within each folder, create another set of classifications according to the special needs or interests of each group, and label tasks as compulsory or voluntary.
- For each subgroup of the class, create a list of compulsory and voluntary websites.

In class

- Demonstrate to students the folders of URLs and any accompanying activities.
- Indicate which website activities are compulsory, which they can choose themselves, and the time they have to complete a set number of tasks.
- Allow a period of time for reporting back on their progress and their levels of satisfaction and/or difficulties they had with the Web-based listening activities.
- Encourage students to focus on the listening skills they have worked on and new language uses they heard.

## Lesson plan requiring students to have Web skills

**Objective:** Students will develop prediction skills for listening to spoken texts on the Web.

**Materials:** Three different spoken texts for the Web, Internet-connected computers.

**Procedure:**

Beforehand

- Find two to three different kinds of spoken texts on the Web, for example, a job interview, a conversation between friends (or strangers), a news report.
- Prepare a rubric that lists the pre-listening activities.

In class

- Show students the different websites containing the listening texts.
- Encourage students to find clues on the website that explain the context for the listening texts.
- Using one text, ask students to focus on clues in the images or other aspects of the website that will help them predict the content of the exchange, for example, number, age, gender, dress style of the people involved.
- Ask students to predict the purpose of the spoken text and some vocabulary items they might expect to hear. Be sure to let students explain their reasons for their predictions.
- Ask students to predict the opening and closing statements or greetings, based on the clues they have just found.
- Ask the class to listen to the text and note which of their predictions they heard.
- Divide the class into two groups. Ask each group to prepare for the second and third texts by repeating the same sequence of activities.
- Compare the groups' predictions. Then allow students to hear the text and judge which predictions were closest.

## Issues to explore

### Issue  Listening online

What kinds of learning tasks and activities help learners to develop listening comprehension skills?

### Exploration – action research

- Keep records of the website audio texts your students listen to and the learning activities they do.
- Ask students to help you evaluate the online listening texts. Ask them to rate them for clarity, usability and relevance to their individual language learning needs.
- Have frequent conversations with students about the listening texts they hear in the classroom and on websites. Discuss their understanding of speakers' meanings.
- Teach students a variety of listening strategies for different kinds of spoken texts, for example: predicting the vocabulary or content of a news item from its headlines; reading news items in a newspaper then listening for these items on TV and radio news; noting the context and participants in a conversation and predicting the content and the level of formality; listening for interaction strategies used by the participants in a conversation.
- Talk to your students about their experiences of listening to real life texts such as television, radio and conversations. Ask them about the strategies they use to hear and learn and how they manage interactions with others.
- Select some of their preferred strategies and allow students to choose them for online and classroom listening texts. Ask them to evaluate how well they worked and why. Keep records of their results. Have students work in pairs and use one of the strategies that their partner selected for a particular activity.
- Introduce your preferred preparation and interaction strategies, explain their purpose, then encourage students to use them when listening to their website texts. Keep records of their results using these strategies.
- At different points of the course, discuss the strategies students have

been using. Compare their results using different kinds of listening strategies. Find out if some strategies work better with particular kinds of listening texts, or whether they use the same strategies for most listening.

- When comparing students' results, note the kinds of preparation and listening strategies preferred at different stages of listening proficiency. For example, do learners at beginner stages find it helpful to read transcripts while listening? Do more advanced learners use this strategy less?

# CHAPTER FOUR

# Reading webpages

As learners develop their ability to retrieve information from the Web, they will learn to expand their literacy skills from reading print-based texts to reading online texts. When students learn how to read and use information on the Web, they will be able to:

- read homepages critically;
- skim and scan a variety of genres;
- evaluate information presented in a variety of genres; and
- synthesise information from several different sites.

While finding and using information on the Web is a useful life skill for second language learners, it also provides opportunities for language learning. As well as skimming and scanning to select texts, they also learn to read a variety of online texts for meaning, some of which are similar in linguistic features to print-based texts, but some of which are specific to the Internet. Additionally, they are challenged to read authentic texts; however, this poses the problems of language level and readability. Our teacher-researchers have found that even advanced second language readers have difficulty reading these new Internet-specific texts if they have no experience with the Web in their home language (Lipscomb 2002). These teachers have found that they need to explicitly teach not only print literacy, but also the digital literacy (Glister 1997) or silicon literacy (Snyder 2002) required to work with and understand the range of new texts on the screen.

*[The CNN homepage] presented no problem to those students familiar with the Internet. However those with poor Internet literacy were 'lost' – unaware of where to look to source the information.*

(Lipscomb 2002: 8)

Usability research has shown that the most common and readable homepages use a three-column format (Nielsen 1998): the centre column containing content, the left column being a table of contents and the right column providing functional links. This research has also found that readable websites chunk information, rather than delivering extended texts in comparable paragraph form to print texts. These chunks may appear as dot points, in boxes, or as short paragraphs. Additionally, websites whose pages are easier to read make use of organisers such as headings or bold or coloured keywords. Websites whose structure is easier to navigate provide limited choices of links that are transparently labelled. No more than two or three clicks beyond the homepage are recommended (Whitbread 2001). Counter-intuitively, the research has also found that graphics do not facilitate reading of webpages. In fact, graphics, video and text compete for our attention and working memory space (Kalyuga 2000; Hoven in press).

> *[Students] entered sites that used first person, past tense, narrative form while they were searching for factual information.* (Mansfield 2002: 3)

Teachers (for example, Lipscomb 2002) have found that they have needed to explicitly teach the structure of webpages through scaffolded activities, especially for learners with no or minimal exposure to the Web in their home language. Such explicit instruction has often been best achieved through print in the classroom, away from the distraction of colour, flashing pop-up windows and the mouse.

In addition to explicit, scaffolded teaching of the structures of Internet-specific texts, teachers have also found that their learners need instruction in how to recognise more standard texts they find on the Web. Since finding appropriate information on the Web requires skimming and scanning, learners need to be able to scan for point of view, genre and other grammatical features (Mansfield 2002). Mansfield, for example, found that his learners did not know how to do this and, as a result, wasted considerable time reading texts that did not provide appropriate information such as factual information compared to personal experience or point of view.

## Teaching suggestions

## Not using email, chat or other CMC

- Using printouts of webpages and screens, demonstrate offline the three-column homepage design, embedded windows, scroll bars and links.

- Then, using a data projector or overhead projector, demonstrate offline the three-column homepage design, embedded windows, scroll bars and links offline.

- Demonstrate frames and non-frames versions of homepages. Show students how to resize frames to make the text easier to read.

- Use printed versions of different texts available on the Web such as narrative and information texts, report and opinion texts. Have learners scan the texts and decide which genre each text is.

- Teach skimming skills. Provide students with URLs that take them to a variety of different genres such as narrative and information texts, report and opinion texts. Have learners skim the texts and decide which genre each text is. Have students compare the reliability of the information from each text. Ask students to list the criteria they used to identify the different genres and also to determine the reliability of the information.

- Teach the features of a particular genre relevant to the course objectives. Have students search the Web for a text of that genre. Ask them to state why their chosen text meets the criteria for the genre.

- Teach the language of argument. Choose a topic of interest to students. Choose a topic for which students will have differing opinions. Divide the class into groups. Source Web texts of different genres on the topic. Assign each group a different text and have them read their text for its information. With whole class, compare the genre and register of each text. Have students write an argument essay on the topic using information from all genres.

- Teach skimming and scanning skills. Source several websites on the same topic but use websites of differing reliability, for example, an advertising site, a university site, a government site, a primary school site. Print out the texts and have students skim and scan the texts in order to compare the information from each text for reliability. With the class, develop criteria for determining reliability of information on the Web. Be sure to include the URL so students can use the information in the URL to help them decide.

- Have students choose an online shopping site, go to it and select items they would like to purchase. Ask them to compare the prices with those at a local store.
- Divide students into groups and have each group choose a university or college they would like to study at. Have them search the site to find out how to apply for a specific degree or course. Have groups compare their findings and decide which has the simplest application process.
- Ask students to choose a topic of interest, for example, movies, Australian animals, restaurants, a country. Ask them to write a report on this topic, using information from at least three different websites.

## Using email, chat or other CMC

- Have students use a search engine to find websites on a chosen topic. Ask them to choose one of the sites, and cut and paste the URL into an email to a classmate, indicating why they think it would be a useful website for the topic.
- Divide students into groups and have each group access a weather site for a different city. Ask groups to collect specific information about the weather in that area, for example, minimum and maximum temperatures, rainfall. Tell groups to email the data they found to each other. Have each group prepare a 'weather report' to present to the class using a presentation program.

## Lesson not using email, chat or other CMC

**Objective:** Students will be able to read information on websites.

**Materials:** Data projector, Internet-connected computers, presentation program.

**Procedure:**

- Brainstorm and list questions students would like to ask about their town or city, such as population, children's holiday activities, festivals.
- From the list, develop a set of questions that are appropriate for searching on the Web.
- Using a data projector, use a search engine to find websites about the town or city.
- With students, choose the websites they want to investigate.
- Divide the class into groups and assign each group a different website.
- Have each group use its website to find as many answers as it can to the questions. Have students write their answers.
- Ask students to compare the answers from the different websites.
- Have groups rate their websites based on the answers they were able to find to the questions.
- Have students categorise the websites according to which is good for what kind of information and what kind of searches.

**Extension:**

- Have students post the answers to the questions on the class webpage.
- Organise students to write the answers to the questions using a presentation program and then present the information to the class using a data projector.
- Encourage students to write to a website if they find errors in the information they collected.

## Lesson not using email, chat or other CMC

**Objective:** Students will be able to determine the reliability of information sourced from different websites.

**Materials:** Internet-connected computers.

**Procedure:**

- With the class, choose a topic of interest.
- Source texts on this topic from several different websites, for example, an advertising site, an elementary school site, a government site, a newspaper, a university site. Print out the texts.
- With the whole class, determine the reliability of each text. As a result of this analysis, develop criteria for determining reliability of information on the Web.
- Source texts from several different websites with information on a different topic.
- Divide the class into groups and give each group a different URL.
- Have each group read the text and determine its reliability, based on the jointly constructed criteria.

**Extension:**

- Have students search the Web for another text on the same topic and determine its reliability.
- Have students compare one of the online texts determined to be reliable with information available in print from a reliable source.

# Lesson not using email, chat or other CMC

**Objective:** Students will be able to read homepages and obtain information from the text.

**Materials:** Homepages with three-column formats, data projector, Internet-connected computers.

## Procedure:

- Choose homepages whose structure follows that recommended by researchers so as not to confuse students at the beginning.
- Print out the homepages and give copies to students.
- Identify the various features of homepages for students, for example, three-column structure, scrollbar, links.
- Ask comprehension questions about the information displayed on the homepage. Include both content information and navigation information, such as menus, links.
- Once students are familiar with the structure of homepages in print, move to the computer.
- Using a data projector, demonstrate the various features of homepages. (Use homepages whose structure follows that recommended by researchers.)
- Ask comprehension questions about the information displayed on the homepage. Include both content information and navigation information, such as menus, links.
- Have students compare reading homepages in print and reading them online. Ask them what is different and what is more difficult and why.

## Extension:

- Have students answer questions about the content of a homepage that does not follow the traditional design. Have them explain what was different and difficult about this task.
- Have students design their ideal homepage and explain why it is ideal.

## Lesson not using email, chat or other CMC

**Objective:**  Students will identify different genres on the Web.

**Materials:**  Internet-connected computers.

**Procedure:**

- Have students choose a topic of interest, for example, movies, Australian animals, restaurants, a country, a festival.
- Search the Web for a variety of genres on this topic, for example, narratives, information texts, opinion texts.
- Divide the class into groups and give each group a different URL.
- Have groups read their text online and identify its genre. Ask them to name the features of the text that led them to identify the genre.
- Have groups report back to the class, summarising the information in their text and describing its generic features.

**Extension:**

- Have students individually write a report on their topic of interest, based on the information gathered from all of the websites.

## Issues to explore

### Issue  Teaching offline

Do students benefit from having particular skills demonstrated offline?

### Exploration – action research

- Provide students with a printout of an Internet-specific text such as homepages or the results of a Web search.
- Teach students the features of the Internet-specific text.
- Have students answer questions about the text. Include questions about navigation as well as about content.
- Observe and take notes on whether students can do the task easily, what questions they ask and what problems they have.
- Using a data projector, teach students the features of another Internet-specific text.
- Ask questions about the text. Include questions about navigation as well as about content.
- Observe and take notes on whether students can do the task easily.
- With the class, decide which demonstration medium is most effective for your learners – print or computer.

### Issue  Scaffolding reading on the Web

Lipscomb (2002) found that she needed to explicitly teach and scaffold for learners how to read texts on the Web, especially for students with minimal or no exposure to the Internet even in their L1.

### Exploration – questions to think about

- Think about your particular learners. What exposure do they have to the Internet in their L1 and in English?
- To what extent do you need to scaffold and explicitly teach your students how to read texts on the Web?

## CHAPTER FIVE

# Content-based instruction

Content-based instruction (CBI) includes approaches to language learning and teaching in which learners engage in a topic of interest or importance to them (Williams 2004) and where the form and sequence of language instruction is dictated by the content. As learners engage in CBI using the Web, they engage in tasks that expand their language and literacy skills, as well as their knowledge of specific content areas relevant to their lives. As a result of CBI (depending on the CBI model used), learners will be able to:

- plan how to use the Web to select information and to communicate with peers or others;
- collaborate and negotiate in English with peers to meet objectives;
- evaluate information on the Web; and
- synthesise information from several different websites.

CBI can be organised in a number of different ways (Brinton, Snow and Wesche 1989) by using:

- themes (such as the law) or topics (such as tenants' rights), often chosen by the students themselves, around which English language instruction is planned;
- adjunct programs where language teachers support learners in discipline-specific courses; and
- sheltered programs where a language teacher teaches the content so that it is accessible to learners who are not fluent in the language.

While the Web can be used in all such programs, its major use is for the first approach and so this will be the focus of this chapter. Themes or topics include a range of different instructional models, from teacher-selected topics to project-based learning. For the former, the Web provides a library of materials from different sources and in different genres from which teachers can select. Many of our teacher-researchers chose, often in collaboration with learners, a topic of interest to explore such as Australian animals (Mansfield 2002), cyclone warnings (Lipscomb 2002),

The Melbourne Cup (King Koi 2002), and job searching (Tun 2002). Even though these researchers found that learners needed to be guided in their search of the Web, once learners could navigate and read the Web (Murray and McPherson 2004), they found themes engaging and therefore motivating (Norton 2002).

Teachers can also use the Web as a source of material for classroom activities that do not require the learners to go online.

Project-based learning, one implementation of CBI, is the use of simulated real-world tasks that are complex and open, ones that challenge learners to think critically and creatively (see, for example, Debski 2005). Project-based learning has been implemented in a variety of educational contexts, with the goal of motivating learners to construct knowledge and link school learning with problems they encounter in the non-educational world. In language teaching, project-based activities provide a bridge between in-class tasks that focus on language learning and using language outside the class (Fried-Booth 1997).

*We were doing letter writing in class. I made the mistake of showing them how to add clip art and borders to create their own stationery. In that instant I lost them. They had great fun experimenting and making Christmas cards.*

(King Koi 2002: 4)

Researchers and teachers have found that learners use language to solve complex problems as they work on their collaborative projects. Computer-based technology provides a mechanism for learners to search and collect the information for their projects and to collaborate with their groups to achieve their goals. Project-based learning needs to be open so that learners can explore their topic in ways that are meaningful to them.

Several steps are critical in project-based learning: choosing a topic, collaboratively planning the project, conducting research, developing a product and evaluating the product. Learners need to be actively involved in each stage. For project-based learning to be more than assigning tasks to students, learners need to be explicitly taught the language skills needed to engage in each step of the process – offering and negotiating topics, planning and negotiating a process, searching and selecting information from the Web, report writing and evaluating language and information. The Internet can be used at any or all of the stages in the project.

Brainstorming can be done via email or on a shared space on a network; planning can be done via email or a discussion list; interviews to gather information can be done via email; data can be gathered from reading information on webpages; reports can be written in the form of a webpage. To utilise the Internet in this way requires explicit teaching of computer skills: presenting reports on a webpage, using Powerpoint to present a report, using email and discussion lists to discuss issues, sending documents as attachments via email and navigating the Web.

> *To my surprise, most students were far more interested in the topic of Australian animals than music, or anything else I could think of.*
> (Mansfield 2002: 2)

## Teaching suggestions

### Not requiring students to have computer skills

(See also Chapter Four for additional suggestions.)

- With the class, brainstorm topics of interest and concern. Then have students vote for the topic they would most like to research.
- With the class, brainstorm topics of interest and concern and have students rank the topics.
- Search the Web for a text on a topic of interest to the class. Use the text for classroom-based activities such as cloze, matching headings to text or having students reassemble a text that has been cut into paragraphs or sentences.
- Choose one topic. Find print-based and Web-based information on the topic and ask students to compare and contrast the information.
- Provide students with printouts of a variety of different genres on their chosen topic from the Web such as narrative and information texts, report and opinion texts. Have learners scan the texts and decide which texts provide the most useful information for their specific project or task.
- Source several different websites on the same topic, but using websites of differing reliability, for example, an advertising site, a university site, a government site, a primary school site. Print out the texts. Have students decide which text provides the most useful information on the topic and then explain why their chosen text is more useful.

### Requiring students to have computer skills

- Teach comparison and contrast language by having students:
  - choose a topic of interest in the current news;
  - read a local newspaper online and then read an online newspaper from their own country (www.onlinenewspapers.com is a useful site to find such newspapers);
  - compare and contrast the news in the local paper with that from their own country;
  - display these similarities and differences using a graphic, for example, a Venn diagram; and

- present their graphic to the class and explain it; or, have the students load their graphic onto the class webpage.
- Teach the language and structure of information texts and have students, in groups:
  - decide on a topic of interest;
  - divide the topic into subtopics so that each student has a subtopic; and
  - search the Web for information on their topic and write an information text on that topic.
- Have students search weather sites for specific cities and monitor their weather over a two-week period. Have students record the information on charts around the room. At the end of the two weeks, ask students to present the data using bar graphs or pie charts, using a wordprocessor or presentation package.
- Organise groups of students to do collaborative projects by sending via email to each other attachments of work they have found on the Web, for example, different information on a project about a particular country or culture or a recent news item.
- Have groups of students do collaborative projects in their field of study by emailing to their classmates attachments of work they have created individually through searching the Web.
- Have students choose a topic and search the Web individually for several sites with information on the topic. Ask students to compare the information from each site on the basis of genre, reliability, accessibility of language and interest level.

## Lesson plans

### Lesson requiring students to have computer skills

**Objective:** Students will be able to retrieve and synthesise information from webpages to complete a joint project.

**Materials:** Internet-connected computers.

**Procedure:**

- Teach the language and structure of information texts.
- Brainstorm a theme of interest to the whole class and then topics within the theme.
- Divide the class into groups and assign a topic to each group within the larger theme. Tell groups how many websites they need to find information from, the types of websites to use, and the length their final information text should be.
- Have each group search the Web for information on their topic.
- Teach students how to summarise information from texts and how to use data from different sources for a written text.
- Have students collaborate in their group offline to write an information text.
- Have students display their information texts around the classroom or in a class folder.

**Extension:**

- Ask groups to post their information texts on the class webpage. With the students' permission, this webpage can be shared with future classes.
- Have groups email their information text to the whole class.
- Have groups compile a list of questions that can be answered from the information in their texts. Have students use the answers to these questions as the outline for their presentation or posting on the website.
- Have the students collate the information from the different groups to create a class text on the theme and its subtopics. This text can be shared with students in another class.

## Lesson using email, chat or other CMC

**Objective:** Students will be able to determine the reliability of information sourced from different websites.

**Materials:** Internet–connected computers.

**Procedure:**

- With the class, choose a topic of interest.
- Source texts on this topic from several websites, for example, an advertising site, an elementary school site, a government site, a newspaper, a university site. Then print them out.
- With the whole class, determine the reliability of each text.
- As a result of this analysis, develop criteria for determining reliability of information on the Web.
- Source texts from several websites with information on another topic.
- Divide the class into groups and give each group a different URL.
- Have each group read the text and determine its reliability based on the jointly constructed criteria.
- Have students decide which of their criteria are more useful than others in determining reliability.

**Extension:**

- Have students search the Web for another text on the same topic and determine its reliability.
- Ask students to compare one of the texts determined to be reliable with a print-based text from a reliable source.

## Lesson not using email, chat or other CMC

**Objective:** Students will be able to use websites to collect and synthesise information.

**Materials:** Internet-connected computers, electronic spreadsheet.

**Procedure:**

- Introduce students to the topic of nutrition.
- Divide the class into groups of five and have students access websites about food and nutrition, a balanced diet and shopping online.
- Ask each group to plan a week's menu for a family of four. Provide the following guidelines about the menu: it must meet nutrition guidelines and must be within a budget assigned by the teacher.
- Have each group prepare the week's budget, using an electronic spreadsheet and using prices from an online shopping site.
- Have groups present their menu and budget to the class.
- Organise the class to vote for the menu that is the most nutritious and economic.
- With students, discuss what language and Internet skills they have learned.

**Extension:**

- Have groups post their menu and budget on the class homepage.

# Lesson using email, chat or other CMC

**Objective:** Students will be able to collaborate on a project in which they retrieve information from the Web, write a report and share information.

**Materials:** Internet-connected computers, presentation program.

**Procedure:**

- Teach the language and structure of reports and the language of interview questions.
- Divide the class into groups and have each group choose a topic for their project. Ask groups to choose a topic people are likely to have opinions about, preferably something of relevance to their local community, for example, city services, community festivals, children's holiday activities, a restaurant.
- Have each student in a group choose one aspect of the topic, for example, restaurant food, service, location.
- Have each student search the Web for a photo and information on their chosen aspect of the topic.
- Based on the information gathered, have students develop a questionnaire about their chosen aspect of the topic.
- Have students conduct interviews with people from the community about their chosen topic, some online via email and others face-to-face.
- Ask each student to copy an appropriate photo and write a report on their particular aspect of the topic, synthesising the information they have gathered from the Web and from their interviews.
- Have groups present their joint project to the class, using a presentation program.

**Extension:**

- Have students post their presentation on the class website.
- Create a book about the topic to share with other classes or people in the community.
- Have different groups create different types of webpages or books for different audiences, for example, for young children, for older beginner ESL learners.

## Issues to explore

### Issue  Project-based learning

Do students benefit from project-based learning?

### Exploration – action research

- Have students engage in a project using the Web that meets the principles of project-based learning (Moss and Van Duzer 1998), which state that project-based learning:
  - builds on previous work;
  - integrates speaking, listening, reading and writing skills;
  - incorporates collaborative team work, problem solving, negotiating and other interpersonal skills;
  - requires learners to engage in independent work;
  - challenges learners to use English in new and different contexts outside the class;
  - involves learners in choosing the focus of the project and in the planning process;
  - engages learners in acquiring new information important to them;
  - leads to clear outcomes; and
  - incorporates self-evaluation, peer and teacher evaluation.
- Observe and take notes on how students collaborate and how they synthesise information. Note particularly how they negotiate, organise and arrive at a consensus.
- Evaluate the language they use to be able to complete this project.
- Decide what students have learned doing this project (language, computer skills and life skills).

## Issue  Content-based instruction

Does working with relevant content motivate students?

## Exploration – questions to think about

- Think about your particular learners. What types of content would motivate them? Why?
- Think about learners in an entirely different context from yours (for example, young learners/adult learners, ESL/EFL, vocational classes/academic preparation classes). What types of content would motivate them? Why?

## CHAPTER SIX

# WebQuests

'WebQuest' is the name given to an instructional model for Web-based learning projects that draw on information and communication resources on the Internet. Originally developed as a means of helping school teachers integrate computer technology into curriculum learning areas (Dodge 1995, 1997; Starr 2000, 2004), WebQuests are now used widely in diverse educational sectors and curriculum areas.

The WebQuest instructional design is based on constructivist principles and is sometimes referred to as inquiry-based learning. The constructivist approach emphasises the role of students as primary agents of learning. Learners engaged in WebQuests find, analyse, classify, synthesise and evaluate information they source on the Internet, and integrate new concepts into established knowledge structures. The originator of WebQuests, Bernie Dodge, describes the concept as 'an inquiry-oriented activity in which most or all of the information used by learners is drawn from the Web' (Dodge 1995: 10).

Teachers have used WebQuests successfully with students of all ages and levels (see, for example, Burleson 2001; Emmert 2003; Joyce and Stohr-Hunt 2004). They design WebQuest projects for students of ESOL (see, for example, Brown 1999), English for Specific Purposes (see, for example, Marco 2002), academic ESL (see, for example, Emmert 2003; Peterson, Caverley and MacDonald 2003), citizenship and social sciences (see, for example, Burleson 2001), literary studies, history, anthropology, mathematics and a range of science subjects (see, for example, Dutt-Doner 2002; Perrone, Clark and Repenning 1996).

TESOL teachers find that WebQuests can broaden their learners' computer and information management skills while furthering language and literacy development. Using a WebQuest framework, students can work individually or in cooperative groups to collect, analyse, and synthesise information sourced from the Internet, then transform it in a variety of different textual forms. Students demonstrate new understandings and knowledge structures while increasing their skills of communication in a variety of spoken and written genres.

WebQuest projects can be tailored to meet individual learner needs or to address specific learning areas. Teachers have reported positive results and achievements for learners who previously demonstrated low levels of motivation, below group norm performances, or social disadvantage (Al-Bataineh, Hamann and Wiegel 2000). Equally, teachers have reported similar results for students who were highly motivated, well-resourced and with substantial experience of using information technologies for learning.

These teachers report that WebQuests engaged learners' interest and motivation, encouraged critical thinking and supported cooperative learning. Working in cooperative learning groups, students improved their spoken language skills through interaction with peers, content experts and community members and improved their writing skills when creating information texts in electronic, print and audiovisual formats.

WebQuest projects are usually designed with a scaffolding framework that helps students navigate through the process, and includes:

- the goals of the WebQuest;
- step-by step guides through the process;
- tasks that structure the development of required skills;
- guides to resources and information; and
- clear descriptions and models of the outcome students must produce.

WebQuests call for careful planning, and interested teachers will find a great deal of information and support to help them on the WebQuest website (http://webquest.sdsu.edu/). This website offers training materials for teachers on how to prepare effective WebQuests and gives many WebQuest examples in a variety of school subject areas, rubrics for evaluating WebQuests and an online template to

*When students are asked to understand, hypothesise or problem-solve an issue that confronts the real world, they face an authentic task, not something that only carries meaning in a school classroom.*
(March 1998)

help teachers plan each stage of their own WebQuest. There is even a professional development activity for groups of teachers that leads them through a process for evaluating WebQuests.

WebQuests can be time-consuming to design. ESOL teachers need to be especially careful that the websites they choose for their students are appropriate for the purpose. They need to be sure that their student teams have the computer, Internet and online literacy skills necessary to undertake WebQuest tasks,

*The answer the student teams develop can be posted, emailed or presented to real people for feedback and evaluation. This authentic assessment motivates students to do their best.* (March 1998)

especially the navigation skills of keeping track of where they are and where they have been. Equally, a well-designed WebQuest should challenge learners to use speaking, listening, reading and writing skills in new and meaningful contexts, while providing opportunities to extend these and develop new skills.

# Teaching suggestions

## Requiring Web skills

- When planning a WebQuest for the first time, consider combining with other classes. It may help to share ideas with other teachers and divide the planning tasks among you.

- Before creating your first WebQuest, review those that are published on the Internet. There might be a WebQuest already available that suits your purposes, or that can be modified to suit your class.

- Key ESL WebQuests into your search engine to find those that focus particularly on language learning. Many well-known ESL websites have a section devoted to WebQuests that have a stronger focus on language than those with a curriculum focus.

- WebQuests can be used to introduce second language learners to Internet-based research. These learners may find search engine results difficult to evaluate, so a WebQuest that has a list of sites already chosen for them will assist them to concentrate on the communication tasks.

- Use ESL WebQuests to teach note-taking, report writing and presentation skills and other academic skills required at the tertiary level. Assessment and evaluation is more manageable when the teacher has chosen the sites and is familiar with the content.

- Teachers can use ESL websites as a basis for WebQuests. Mature learners can learn to evaluate their individual learning needs by selecting and evaluating the learning resources on these sites, then reporting to the whole class on their effectiveness. In doing this, they will become familiar with the language learning resources on the Internet while developing independent learning skills and increasing their experience of using ESL resources on the Internet.

- When planning WebQuests, think carefully about how students will report their results. Ensure they all have opportunities to present their findings in ways that enhance their speaking and writing skills.

- For adolescent and young adult learners, WebQuests can be a fun way to explore topics of interest to their age group. They can explore websites for sports, music and arts while developing critical thinking skills and exploring attitudes and values and how language is used to express these.

- For some learners it may be useful to include tasks that require them to evaluate the authenticity of information on some websites. As learners mature in their use of the Internet, they can learn not only how to evaluate the quality of information on the website, but also the features of the site that indicate the reliability of the information (see also Chapter Two).

- WebQuests can be useful for adult learners living in new communities. They can explore unfamiliar cultural norms and practices with their classmates and critically analyse their meanings.

- When your students have experienced some WebQuests and are familiar with the procedures, allow them to design one for another class group to complete.

# Lesson plans

## Lesson to familiarise students with WebQuests

**Objective:** Students will identify and describe community services available to immigrants in their geographic area.

**Materials:** Internet-connected computers.

**Procedure:**

- Have a class discussion about the kinds of services needed by immigrants in their first 12 months in the country and those that students are familiar with.

- Discuss students' experiences of seeking these services, the spoken and written interactions they experienced and the role language played in the success or difficulty of these interactions.

- Give students a simple description of WebQuests.

- Explain that the goals of this WebQuest are to: identify the kinds of services available to immigrants in the local area; identify any gaps in these services; and learn and use new language skills to interact with local people and community service organisations in order to locate and use services.

- Design a rubric to evaluate students' language, communication and research skills. (See http://webquest.sdsu.edu/ for help with rubrics.) Ensure students have this rubric for reference from the beginning.

- Organise resources such as: a list of URLs of useful websites, or if creating a class website for their WebQuest, include a page of links to relevant organisations; a list of community organisations in the area on the class website or in print; a local community services directory, if available; Yellow pages telephone books, especially of the local area; guest speakers from local community service organisations; and visits to local child care centres, health centres, aged services centres.

- Divide the class into small teams or allow students to organise their own teams. Have each team choose a group in the community service to focus on, for example, preschool children's services, school age children's services, adult groups, family groups, or people interested in particular sports and hobbies.

- Have each team identify the needs of their chosen community group by carrying out surveys and interviews with their classmates, friends, family and others, for example.
- Ask teams to find the organisations, groups and people who offer these services and then locate and make contact with them. Have teams get information about the services they currently offer by using the resources you have provided (see the previous page).
- Have teams report to the class on their findings on the range of services available to their chosen community group. Allow students to choose from a range of reporting options, for example: flowcharts, maps and diagrams; Powerpoint presentations; webpages; written reports. Provide links to these models on the Internet or in classroom resource materials. Ask guest speakers to use these models, where possible and model these yourself in your lessons.

**Extension:**

- Have students evaluate the range of services available and identify gaps based on their needs analysis survey and the group reports.
- Ask students to describe issues of cultural sensitivity that might arise from people using (or not using) community services.
- Have students list issues that arose from the perspectives of community service providers, for example, access to funding, extent of reach into their constituency.
- Ask students to evaluate their language experiences, difficulties that arose and the strategies they used to overcome them.

# Issues to explore

## Issue  Communication skills

When gathering information for WebQuests, your students may need to interview people in the community, or request certain kinds of information. How well prepared are they for these communication activities? What spoken discourse skills do students need in order to request information in spoken exchanges?

## Exploration – action research

- Teach students the discourse structures of transactional interactions.
- Have students list the information they need from a community group they wish to approach.
- Ensure students are familiar with essential vocabulary related to the organisation and its services.
- Audit students' spoken discourse skills, for example, openings and closings; requests for repetition, clarification and feedback; and turn-taking.
- Have students rehearse with you. Challenge their skills by feigning misunderstanding, terseness and other responses.
- Ask students to try out their skills by making requests for information from your school office.
- Evaluate the results of the trial: did they return with the appropriate information and experience success, or did they have difficulty? Ask the school office member to give you and the students constructive feedback.
- In your teaching, prioritise the discourse features that were most problematic.

## Issue  Reading strategies for print-based and Web-based texts

WebQuest activities usually involve a great deal of reading from webpages. Do print-based information texts and Web-based reading texts require the same kinds of reading skills and strategies?

## Exploration – action research

- Give your students a print-based text on a familiar topic in a familiar genre to read.
- Give your students the URL of a website text of similar length, genre and level of reading difficulty, and on the same topic.
- Assess students' comprehension of both texts. Use the same comprehension assessment strategy for both texts, for example, design a flowchart, draw a picture, answer questions. Be sure that the answers can only be drawn from one of the texts, not both.
- Analyse the results. Are they the same across both texts? Do some students display different reading abilities across the two texts? If so, talk to the students about the reasons for the difficulty and plan future reading lessons that address the differences.

## Issue  Language learning using WebQuests

Exploration – questions to think about

- What kinds of Web-reading skills do students need in order to locate information in Web-based reading texts?
- What kinds of written language skills do students need to request information by email from community organisations?
- How do we evaluate the language gains students achieve through their experiences in WebQuests?

## CHAPTER SEVEN

# Learning management systems

Web-based learning management systems such as WebCT, Blackboard, LAMS (Learning Activity Management System: see http://www.melcoe.mq.edu.au/projects/lams.htm), eBoard and Lotus LMS (formerly Learning Space) bring together communicating on the Internet (McPherson and Murray 2003) and the delivery of content in an online environment. These systems can be used to support face-to-face instruction or for complete online distance learning. In either case, such systems help learners to:

- participate in a course from a distance or at their convenience;
- collaborate and negotiate in English with peers to meet objectives; and
- review course content in their own time.

In addition, they can help teachers reflect on both the product and process of learning (Johnson 2003) because student interactions can be captured and archived. They help teachers integrate the Web as an information source with teacher-produced materials and with interactive online communication. Also, they provide the opportunity for individualised instruction to meet the needs of disparate learners in the same class (King Koi 2002). However, such advantages come at a considerable cost of time to develop a seamless online learning environment tailored to the specific learning objectives of their learners (see, for example, Palloff and Pratt 1999).

*Preparation is the same as for any multi-level class – extremely time consuming and challenging but also extremely rewarding.*
(King Koi 2002: 4)

Most commercially available learning management systems include tools such as chat, email, discussion lists, tracking of student progress, auto-marked tests, calendars, individual student homepages or work areas, group project organisation, course content pages and systems for collecting and collating student marks. Some systems also have audio capabilities. Most teachers who use systems such as WebCT make use of the threaded discussion tool on topics in the course content.

*I also think it [online discussion] saves time in that it gives students more time to process, question, and get feedback as opposed to just being in a classroom setting.*

(Dabbagh 2002)

All research and advice on using a learning management system (LMS) notes that merely uploading information directly from print text onto the Web is not appropriate and does not facilitate student learning. Rather, the most effective use of content delivery is with the addition of interactive activities for learners to respond to. Since these are not automatically built into the system, they require additional computer programming skills on the part of the teacher or the institution, as well as advice from instructional designers. However, most of these systems are only available at the institutional level.

Open source systems such as Stanford University's CourseWork (http://coursework.stanford.edu/) or simpler systems such as eBoard (http://www.eboard.com/) have fewer tools, but are more readily available for teachers and simpler to upload information to. Most open source systems do not have built-in communication tools so that the teacher has to link to communication tools such as email, rather than it being an integrated part of the LMS. One of our teacher-researchers (King Koi 2002) used eBoard as the online environment for all her online class activities. This system uses a corkboard with post-it notes to display the table of contents. Over several semesters, King Koi developed a series of modules, which were 'a collection of Internet sites for students to access easily and quickly' (page 2). Each module was on a specific theme such as ESL sites, Australia, study/work, each of which had subtopics such as study skills, job search skills, resumés. Then, under each subtopic was a list of links to appropriate websites. In this way, she, as teacher, selected the websites for her students to visit, thus alleviating the problem of students finding inappropriate sites. Since the site she constructed was password-protected, students were able to post their own messages to share with their class and often with future classes.

One open source LMS, Moodle (http://moodle.org), has been developed by an educator based on social constructivist pedagogy and is contributed to by many language teachers. This system provides interactivity in teacher-created activities (such as drag-and-drop matching), video and audio features, as well as the more usual LMS features such as chat, discussion lists, and quiz tools.

## Teaching suggestions

### Requiring online and face-to-face interaction

- Using a data projector, demonstrate the drafting and editing tools that allow students to undo errors or make changes to their messages on the class discussion site, and how to post messages to threads. Allow students time to practise and encourage them to check that the message appears as they intended.

- Using a data projector, demonstrate how to delete messages on a discussion list.

- Divide the class into groups and have each group work on an oral presentation. Have students within each group share documents and other resources online to produce their presentation. Get each group to present their presentation online.

- In groups, have students discuss a topic of interest or one that is part of the course content. Have each group summarise their discussion and post their summary onto the class discussion list.

- Set a writing task and ask students to post their drafts to the student work area on the LMS. Put students in pairs and provide a rubric for students to evaluate their partner's paper for homework. Have students provide feedback to their partners in class.

- Choose a topic that meets course goals and divide it into subtopics. Load content or links to webpages on each subtopic on the LMS. Divide the class into groups and assign each group a task related to its subtopic. Ask students within each group to complete the task by interacting in group discussion lists online. Have students present their completed task orally to the class.

- Have students choose a topic about which they have different views. Divide the class into groups and have each group discuss the topic in class. Record the discussions and transcribe sections of the discussions. Repeat the activity using another topic but have students conduct the discussions on the discussion list of the LMS. Print out the discussion. Have students compare the language used online with the language used in face-to-face discussions.

- Have students choose a topic and prepare an oral presentation on the topic. When students do their presentations, use an LMS with audio capability. Upload the audio files for peer comment to the class webpage. Provide students with detailed criteria for peer comment.

## Requiring online interaction only

- Divide the class into groups and have each group work on a presentation using the discussion list tool of an LMS. Have students share documents and other resources online to produce their presentation by pasting them to the class shared area of the LMS. Get them to load their presentation onto the class shared area in the LMS. This can also be done with audio, rather than print, if the LMS has audio capability.
- Set a writing task and ask students to post their drafts to the class shared area on the LMS. Put students in pairs and provide a rubric for students to evaluate their partner's paper for homework. Have students provide feedback to their partner via the email tool.
- Have students practise summarising by:
  - loading content or links to websites onto the class shared space on the LMS;
  - dividing the class into groups and allocating different content to each group;
  - getting groups to access their content on the class shared area; and
  - having groups use a group online forum to prepare a summary of their content and then paste it in the class shared area.

## Lesson plans

### Lesson requiring students to have computer skills

**Objective:** Students will be able to collaborate online to produce a group presentation.

**Materials:** Internet-connected computers, an LMS.

**Procedure:**

- Teach the linguistic features of a report.
- Teach the language of agreement and disagreement and of negotiation that would be appropriate for an online forum.
- As a class, choose a topic of interest to the class and then brainstorm different subtopics of this topic.
- Divide the class into groups and assign each group a different subtopic.
- Upload content and links to websites on each of the subtopics.
- Have students read the content on the LMS and then link to several websites.
- Using an online forum, have students negotiate to write a report on their subtopic for presentation to the whole class.
- Have students present their report on the class shared space on the LMS.

**Extension:**

- Have students attach photos from webpages to their reports.
- Organise students to send their reports to other class members.

# Lesson requiring students to have computer skills

**Objective:** Students will be able to identify and use different genres in online discussions.

**Materials:** Internet-connected computers, an LMS, a printout of a threaded discussion list conversation.

## Procedure:

Part 1 – offline

- Analyse a threaded discussion list conversation with the whole class, helping students to identify the markers inserted automatically by the computer program (for example, **From:**) or through choice by the sender (for example, >>> to represent different turns).

- Divide the class into groups and assign each group a different topic. Ensure the topics range from very personal to abstract so students will write in a variety of genres, for example, narrative, recount, report, argument. Pre-teach the features of the different genres if necessary.

Part 2 – online

- Have students post their responses to the assigned topic to their group's discussion list; ensure that the discussion list has been adjusted so it reports threads based on topic.

- Have students print out their group's conversation and identify turns and genre features.

Part 3 – offline

- With the whole class, compare turn-taking and genre features in the different discussions.

- Work with students to develop a 'theory' of how the context shapes the generic features of texts.

- Have groups exchange their discussions so that a group that wrote narratives exchanges with a group that wrote reports; have groups choose one posting and rewrite in a different genre.

## Extension:

- Have students compare the generic features of their discussion list postings with a set of their in-class print writing. Help students analyse the differences so they can see that it is the context that shapes the text, rather than the medium.

# Lesson requiring students to have computer skills

**Objective:** Students will be able to use appropriate language in online discussions.

**Materials:** Internet-connected computers, an LMS, tape recorder.

**Procedure:**

Part 1 – offline

- Divide the class into groups of five and assign each group a different topic about which people have varying opinions.
- Have each group discuss their topic in class. Record each group's discussion and transcribe short sections of each discussion, especially ones around language features taught, for example, agreeing and disagreeing.

Part 2 – online

- Assign each group another topic about which people have varying opinions.
- Have each group discuss the topic in the online discussion of the LMS.
- Print out the online discussions.

Part 3 – offline

- In class, have each group compare the linguistic features of their face-to-face discussion with their online discussion.
- Have each group list the similarities and differences in linguistic features of the online and face-to-face discussions.

Part 4 – online

- Ask each group to paste their findings on the class shared space of the LMS.
- Have each group compare the findings of other groups with their own, using the online discussion tool.

**Extension:**

- Ask the class to develop a list of linguistic features of discussions for both online and face-to-face modes to be posted on the class webpage.

## Issues to explore

### Issue  The effectiveness of learning management systems

Do students benefit from learning via a learning management system?

### Exploration – action research

- Observe a colleague using WebCT or another system; 'lurk' on the online student discussion in that colleague's class.
- Interview the colleague about the kinds of activities she has students engage in, their level of engagement, their language development and the time it takes for her to work with learners online.
- Observe one of your own classes. Take notes on the kinds of activities students engage in, their level of engagement, their language development and the time it takes for you to prepare and respond to student learning.
- Determine which tools on the learning management system are the most effective for student learning.
- Develop a course for your students using the tool you deem most effective.
- Observe and take notes on student engagement and learning and your own time spent on the course.
- Continue this cycle until you have determined which learning management system tools support learning and which add too much to the teacher's workload.

### Issue  Should students do courses entirely online?

Is the most appropriate use of learning management systems as an adjunct to face-to-face instruction or as a delivery mechanism for an entire course?

### Exploration – questions to think about

- Think about your particular learners. Which mode best suits their needs? Why?
- Think about which types of learners could benefit from an entirely online delivered course. Why would they benefit?

## Issue Flexibility

Vazquez (2002) quotes a teacher who changed his lesson plan to take advantage of a 'learning moment'.

## Exploration – questions to think about

- What advice do you have for other teachers about how to be flexible to take advantage of unexpected events resulting from online teaching?
- How can teacher education and professional development programs teach such flexibility?

CHAPTER EIGHT

# Creating webpages

When the Internet became more widely available to language teaching schools and programs, ESL/EFL teachers saw possibilities for language teaching and learning that went beyond information seeking, communicating by email, chat, MOOs and MUDs.

Some teachers saw opportunities for developing students' writing skills with the Web's function as 'publisher'. The Web's open environment allows any individual to publish their own materials, and language teachers were quick to see the motivational effects of publishing students' own work on the Web. One advantage of publishing on the Web is its immediacy. Students can see their work published virtually as soon as it is written. And after the materials have been published students can continue to edit, amend and update their work at any time, with ease.

Early adopters quickly developed skills in writing Hypertext Markup Language (html), the programming script for the World Wide Web. They taught their ESL students to write simple webpages in html for personal and class websites.

Now, Web-authoring can easily be done by students at any level of second language proficiency and even with elementary computer skills. Teachers are discovering that Web editors bundled with commercial wordprocessing applications have simplified the task enormously.

Teachers and students who consider themselves not proficient with html can be guided through a Web editor by its tutorial, allowing more attention to the design of language tasks and texts to be published and avoiding the technicalities of manually writing html and uploading files (Endres 2002).

Teacher webpages are a useful way to collect and collate resources and materials for students and for directing students towards resources that will facilitate their learning. In her class, King Koi (2002) prepares a webpage with links to resources that help her students achieve the learning tasks assigned at each lesson. As well as links to ESL sites, she has tutorials for letter-writing, puzzles and games, online newspapers, dictionaries, and TV and radio sites. She creates a class information section in which she and students can upload personal information for each other, for example, photographs, messages, and announcements. Her site is password-protected so only she and her students can access it from the ISP hosting it.

*My pages therefore are not an electronic version of the printed page, but contain elements that reflect an understanding of the language learning and acquisition process.*

(Puetter 2002)

Puetter (2002) describes a different model for a class webpage. He creates a language learning webpage in which students link from his page to an online story or article in the local newspaper. Students use interactive functions on his purpose-built site to link to the article, locate a set of comprehension questions, and record their responses. He finds that by designing his own webpages he can marry students' two main needs of content and language development.

*I became curious as to ways my students could use the Internet more as a means of communication. Could I make the communication via the Internet more 'two-way'? How could my students 'send' as well as 'receive' information via the Internet?*

(Endres 2002)

Soltesz (1996) taught html to his second-year engineering students in an English for Academic Purposes course so they could create their own webpages on which to publish their reports and assignments. He reported that the students were very motivated to create attractive webpages and took great pains with their grammar, syntax and spelling as well as with the design of their websites.

When Endres (2002) suggested to the students in his ESL writing class that they publish their own biographies on a student webpage, at first they 'couldn't see the point'. Why would anyone want to read their page? Who would read it? What was so interesting about them? However, when completing a questionnaire at the end of the course, 75 per cent of students said their computer skills had improved a lot and 62 per cent stated their English skills had improved a lot. Webpage activities were nominated as a particularly useful part of the course.

Teachers planning to begin Web-authoring for themselves or their class may find the advice of more experienced TESOL colleagues helpful. They recommend using website design principles that take into account the needs of the user or reader (Fox 1998; Kelly 2000; Burch 2001; Nielsen 2002). They advise teachers to be very familiar with software before embarking on projects with students (Endres 2002) and emphasise that they should give their first priority to the design of good language learning activities and tasks.

> *The students with more advanced (computer) knowledge used their understanding to circumvent L2 difficulties by using the Ctrl+F function to locate vocabulary on the page rather than scanning for textual information, and by cutting and pasting sentences rather than writing them.*
> (Puetter 2002)

Some teachers report that class webpages help to manage large classes, especially when collecting student assignments and giving feedback (see, for example, King Koi 2002). Many report that students who previously disliked writing tasks became more motivated and produced better quality work.

Students and teachers report that an additional benefit of using class websites to develop language skills has been improved computer skills and these they valued as important educational skills to acquire (Endres 2002; Kong Koi 2002).

# Teaching suggestions

## Requiring no Web skills

- Ease students into an understanding of the versatile nature of website publishing by creating a class website on the school Intranet or on a private site. Create two to three pages of classwork information, photos and short biographies of staff and students. Update it regularly so students become familiar with the notion of the changing nature of Web-based information.

- When planning out of class excursions, take along a camera and take photos of interesting sights, events and student activities. As a class activity, have students write short descriptive pieces about the photos and publish them on the website.

- Ask students to bring in their own photos and interesting pieces of information or stories. Encourage them to write about them in their own words and publish them on the website.

- When students are reluctant to write and publish their own biographies, brainstorm other topics of interest such as your school history, local sites of interest, favourite sports and sports heroes, an interesting job.

- Encourage students interested or skilled in design to suggest new layouts, colour schemes, font styles and so on. Show these students how to change the design features of the class website and allow them to take turns in displaying their different design styles.

- Over time, encourage students to take responsibility for the design and editing of the class website. Some may prefer the writing tasks while others may become involved in design and navigation styles.

- Start reluctant writers by involving them in group writing tasks where all contribute a short piece to begin with. Ensure they choose topics they are interested in and gradually increase the requirements for length and complexity as a condition of publication on the website.

- Discuss issues of privacy with students, and the difference between publishing material on the World Wide Web for all to see and of publishing on a protected class site which only they can view.

- Explain issues of copyright and the hazards or bad manners of copying and pasting from other people's sites.
- Encourage students to go outside the class to get information for their website. They can interview other students, class guest speakers, members of the local community or local politicians. Keeping the information to local issues helps to give the site a 'community' feel.

## Requiring Web skills

- Organise students into teams with responsibilities for the website. The more technically minded students can learn to create navigation links and upload files; some can be responsible for eliciting contributions from classmates or other people; and others can have an editorial role and proofread items selected for publication.
- Ask students to view and evaluate other class websites in your institution or those they have found on the Web. Discuss the kinds of information they find interesting and useful and what ideas it generates for their own website.
- To get students into the habit of checking their site, have a regular class activity in which you view the website together, discuss the new items, and elicit new ideas for making the site interesting and effective. Let them see you make editorial changes 'on the spot' to show how easily it can be done.
- Think about making links with another class in another part of the country or overseas. It will increase your students' motivation to know that another class reads their website. And for your class, visiting another class's website gives them reading opportunities on a website that is at their language level and their level of interest.

## Lesson plans

### Lesson plan not requiring students to have Web skills

**Objective:** Students will participate in planning a class website.

**Materials:** List of class websites, data projector, evaluation sheet, Internet-connected computers.

**Procedure:**

- Before class, review a variety of school or class websites. Choose those suited to your purposes and create a page of links to the sites. Add two or three more than necessary in order to compensate for any that fail during class time.

- Divide the class into groups of three or four and send each group an email with links to your selected websites.

- Before students access the websites, use a data projector to demonstrate each website to students. Draw attention to the source, authors, date, and other kinds of information about the site.

- Design an evaluation sheet for students to comment on features and design of the websites, for example, the kinds of information on a site, how interesting they find the site, how readable it is and how well it uses images, colour and design features (see also Chapter Four).

- Have students use the evaluation sheet for each website.

- Ask each group to give a short verbal report on what they saw and liked best on each website and the reasons for their rating.

- Ask groups to put the reports together and draw up a priority list of publishing and design recommendations for their class website. Discuss the feasibility of the recommendations and agree on which ones they will use for their class website.

- Discuss copyright issues and plagiarism and how to acknowledge sources when others' materials are used.

- Discuss who will take on different roles and responsibilities for the class website. A minimum requirement should be that all students contribute some written work. Writing tasks can be adapted to a variety of literacy levels, for example, students at beginner literacy levels can prepare captions for images or alphabetise lists, while others can write opinion pieces, stories or reports.

# Lesson plan requiring students to have Web skills

**Objective:** Students will create their own biographic webpages.

**Materials:** Internet-connected computers, Web editor.

**Procedure:**

- Discuss with students the purposes and readership of personal webpages and the kinds of information that make them interesting to others.
- Divide the class into groups and ask them to discuss the design of a template for personal webpages. Ask them to think about the kinds of information they should include, the appropriate length of text and the use of images that would be suitable for personal webpages.
- Discuss the design with students and the cultural meanings behind colour, patterns, font styles and sizes.
- Distribute the agreed template to students and allow them to add one piece of personal information.
- Show students how to use the design tools on the Web editor and encourage them to play with colours, patterns, font style and other tools to design their personal pages.
- Ask students to begin preparing texts to be uploaded on their sites. Establish a protocol for proofreading and editing, either as a collaborative activity or with final proofing by a teacher. Encourage students to use dictionaries, a thesaurus and grammar manuals to check their work.
- Plan a webpage launch. When students introduce their page, have them describe how and why they made design decisions and why they wrote particular texts.
- Encourage students to update and review their sites on a regular basis to keep them fresh, relevant and interesting.

## Issues to explore

### Issue   Using Web publishing to improve writing skills

Many teachers report on the motivational effects of having students write for the class website. They say that students demonstrate a renewed interest in writing tasks and pay close attention to editing and proofreading their own work. While increasing the frequency and quantity of writing output, students may also use their language skills in more complex and creative ways. Does Web publishing lead to improvements in students' writing skills?

### Exploration – action research

- Select a small number of students whose written work you will monitor over the period of a course in which they write for the class website.
- Take notes on the writing tasks they do. Note how many they complete, the genres they use in their writing and the size of the text. Ask about their attitudes to writing tasks, for example, do they enjoy writing or find it a chore?
- Develop a protocol of language skills you want to monitor, for example, use of single or multiclause sentences, use of tense, punctuation, paragraphing.
- Take notes on the number of consultations you have with the students and the kinds of assistance you provide.
- At the end of the course compare their early writing samples with later work. Examine the variety of genres they used, the size of the texts and the complexity of the language they used.
- Discuss the results of your findings with your students. Ask how they feel about writing and if their attitudes have changed.

# Glossary of computer terms

| | |
|---|---|
| append | include a previous email attached to the current one |
| attachment | a document sent along with an email |
| banner | a graphic image on a website, usually for advertising |
| Blackboard | a suite of software for online teaching and learning that integrates teaching, learning, student services and back office systems |
| bookmarking | saving an URL for future use; clicking on the bookmark takes the user to the URL; used for frequently visited websites so the URL doesn't have to be entered each time |
| Boolean operators | terms that narrow searches, such as *and, or, not* |
| browser | a program such as Explorer or Netscape that allows the user to browse the World Wide Web |
| CBI | content-based instruction |
| chat | synchronous written communication between people who are logged onto computers that are networked |
| click | press and release a button on the mouse to start an activity such as opening a webpage |
| clip art | computerised art or graphics available online to be imported into a document |
| CMC | computer-mediated communication: communication between people using computer networks; CMC includes email, chat, instant messaging and discussion lists |
| computer network | computers linked together so that files and messages can be sent from one to the other |

| | |
|---|---|
| CourseWork | an open source learning management system available from Stanford University |
| data projector | an electronic projector for displaying images from computers onto a screen |
| directory | an online tool that helps users find sites on the Web; organised by topic/theme |
| discussion list | asynchronous communication where many people 'post' messages to be read by everyone with access to the discussion list |
| eBoard | An LMS that allows teachers to post information and links for student access |
| email | written messages sent asynchronously across a computer network; email can be sent to one or many people if you know their email addresses |
| email account | a personal account for sending email; email accounts can be with an email client, either through a stand-alone client or an Internet Service Provider |
| email address | an address for people to send your email to; includes userid and the server you are using to connect you to the network |
| file | a computer document with a name (given by the writer); a set of data stored on a computer |
| forum | group online discussion |
| genre | a staged, culturally specific text with specific organisational and linguistic structures; sometimes also called a text type. |
| homepage | first screen (page) of a website |
| hostname | unique name by which a computer is identified on a network |
| hot link | highlighted area on a Web page; a hyperlink to other sites or documents |

| | |
|---|---|
| html | Hypertext Markup Language, the programming script for the World Wide Web |
| hyperlink | a way to link text or other information in a Web-like, rather than a linear, manner |
| icon | an image that represents a concept, for example, a closed envelope to represent an unread email message |
| Internet | a network of computer networks that links computers around the world; often abbreviated to 'Net' |
| Intranet | a private network inside an organisation that uses the same kinds of software that you would find on the Internet, but it is only for internal use |
| ISP | Internet Service Provider, a company that provides access to the Internet for a fee |
| LAMS | Learning Activity Management System: a tool for designing, managing and delivering online collaborative learning activities; available through Macquarie University |
| LMS | learning management systems: an LMS brings together communicating on the Internet and the delivery of content in an online environment. Examples include WebCT, Blackboard, LAMS, eBoard and Lotus LMS. |
| login | a protocol used for opening an email account or a computer that is connected to a network |
| Lotus LMS | an integrated system that manages classroom-based and e-learning resources, courseware and events |
| MOO | Multi-object-oriented MUDs: one of several kinds of multi-user role-playing environments |
| MUD | Multi-User Dungeon or Dimension: an interactive virtual game played on the Internet by several people at the same time. Some are for entertainment, others for serious software development or educational purposes |

| | |
|---|---|
| moodle | an open source learning management system with a constructionist pedagogy |
| navigate | to find a route through hyperlinks and commands or other online pointers in software or on the Web |
| offline | working without a computer or with a computer that is not currently connected live to a network |
| online | working on a computer that is actively connected to a network |
| open source | software available free to users |
| password | private identification for a computer system to identify a person; a userid is also needed; the password is to protect people's information and should not be shared with anyone else |
| pop-up | a graphic or text in a small window that jumps off the screen to attract attention; often used for advertising |
| post | add a comment to a discussion list |
| pull-down menu | a menu of choices that can be found by clicking a computer mouse over a header on a computer screen |
| scrolling | using the mouse to move up or down the document to see information beyond what is on the viewable screen |
| search engine | an online tool that helps users find sites on the Web by searching for key words or phrases |
| server | a computer that links one computer to another |
| threaded discussion | discussion in which all postings to the same topic are linked |
| upload | move a document from a wordprocessor or spreadsheet to an online space |
| URL | Uniform Resource Locator: the address for a website or other Internet facility |

| | |
|---|---|
| userid (username) | identification (name) used for a computer system and communicators to identify a person; used for many accounts and systems; a password is also required |
| WebCT | a learning management system (LMS) designed principally for higher education institutions |
| Web editors | computer programs for designing and creating webpages |
| webpage | a document housed on a server on the World Wide Web |
| website | a collection of files/documents on a specific subject, housed on a server connected to the World Wide Web; the website is identified in the hostname section of the URL |
| windows | the frame in which one section of information is presented; different pages can be displayed in different windows on the computer screen at the same time |
| wordprocessor | a computer program that helps people write, using a computer |
| World Wide Web | a hyperlinked database residing on the Internet, providing network-accessible information in text, graphics, video and audio formats |

# Bibliography

Below is a list of readings referred to in the text or references for further reading on the topic. In addition, teachers can find an extensive listing of ESL/TESOL websites where they can locate additional activities at the NCELTR resource centre:

http://www.nceltr.mq.edu.au/eslsites.html

Readers might also want to access some of the online help available that provides tips for using search engines such as:

http://www.nceltr.mq.edu.au/pdamep/wrs2/default.htm
http://searchenginewatch.com/facts/index.php
http://webresearch.webpower.nl
http://www.learnthenet.com/english/index.html
http://www.learnwebskills.com/search/main.html

## Series introduction

Burns, A. (1995). Teacher researchers: Perspectives on teacher action research and curriculum renewal. In A. Burns & S. Hood (Eds.), *Teachers' voices: Exploring course design in a changing curriculum* (pp. 3–19). Sydney: NCELTR.

Edge, J. (Ed.). (2001). *Action research*. Case studies in TESOL series. Alexandria, VA: TESOL.

Freeman, D. (1998). *Doing teacher research: From inquiry to understanding*. Boston: Heinle & Heinle Publishers.

Hoven, D. (1999). CALL-ing the learner into focus: Towards a learner-centred model. In R. Debski & M. Levy (Eds.), *World CALL: Global perspectives on computer-assisted language learning* (pp. 149–168). Lisse: Swets & Zeitlinger Publishers.

Kemmis, S., & McTaggart, R. (Eds.). (1988). *The action research planner* (3rd ed.). Geelong: Deakin University Press.

Snyder, I. (2002). *Silicon literacies*. London: Routledge.

Wallace, M. (1998). *Action research for language teachers*. Cambridge: Cambridge University Press.

# Introduction

Bachman, L. F., & Palmer, A. S. (1996). *Language testing in practice: Designing and developing useful language tests*. Oxford: Oxford University Press.

Blatnik, B. (2002). *ESL listening resources*. Unpublished action research report, AMEP Research Centre, Sydney, Australia.

Hammond, J. (Ed.). (2001). *Scaffolding: Teaching and learning in language and literacy education*. Newtown, Australia: Primary English Teaching Association.

King Koi, N. (2002). *Using the Internet in the AMEP classroom with multi-level classes*. Unpublished action research report, AMEP Research Centre, Sydney, Australia.

Kress, G. (1997). Visual and verbal modes of representation in electronically mediated communication: The potentials of new forms of text. In I. Snyder (Ed.), *Page to screen: Taking literacy into the electronic era* (pp. 53–79). Sydney: Allen & Unwin.

Lipscomb, P. (2002). *Reading what? on the Web*. Unpublished action research report, AMEP Research Centre, Sydney, Australia.

Little, D., Devitt, S., & Singleton, D. (1994). The communicative approach and authentic texts. In A. Swarbrick (Ed.), *Teaching modern languages* (pp. 43–47). London: Routledge.

Norton, P. (2002). *Using Internet resources in the AMEP*. Unpublished action research report, AMEP Research Centre, Sydney, Australia.

Mansfield, S. (2002). *Taming and teaching the Internet in the English language classroom*. Unpublished action research report, AMEP Research Centre, Sydney, Australia.

Murray, D. E. (2003). Materials for new technologies: Learning from research and practice. In W. A. Renandya (Ed.), *Methodology and materials design in language teaching* (pp. 30–43). Singapore: SEAMEO Regional Language Centre.

Puetter, S. (2002). *Using the Internet in the classroom*. Unpublished action research report, AMEP Research Centre, Sydney, Australia.

Snyder, I. (1999). Digital literacies: Renegotiating the visual and the verbal in communication. *Prospect*, 14(3), 13–23.

Snyder, I. (2002). *Silicon literacies*. London: Routledge.

Sutherland-Smith, W. (2002). Web-text: Perceptions of digital reading skills in the ESL classroom. *Prospect*, 17(1), 55–70.

Tindale, J. (in press). Reading print and electronic texts. In D. E. Murray & P. McPherson (Eds.), *Navigating to read; reading to navigate*. Sydney, Australia: NCELTR.

Unat, H. (2002). *Using Internet resources in the AMEP: How to utilise ESL websites in the classroom*. Unpublished action research report, AMEP Research Centre, Sydney, Australia.

Vazquez, M. A. (2002). *Integrating the Internet in language teaching: Personal and institutional factors*. Unpublished M.App.Ling. thesis, Macquarie University, Sydney, Australia.

Warschauer, M. (1999). *Electronic literacies: Language, culture, and power in online education*. Mahwah, NJ: Erlbaum.

Warschauer, M., Turbee, L., & Roberts, B. (1994). *Computer learning networks and student empowerment*. (Research Note #10). Honolulu, HI: University of Hawaii, Second Language Teaching and Curriculum Centre.

## Chapter 1

Baharlou, A. (2002). *Using Internet resources in the AMEP*, Unpublished action research report, AMEP Research Centre, Sydney, Australia.

Ginsberg, L. (1998). Integrating technology into adult learning. Technology, basic skills, and adult education: Getting ready and moving forward. ERIC Information Series No. 375. Columbus, OH: ERIC Clearinghouse on Adult, Career, and Vocational Education.

Mansfield, S. (2002). *Taming and teaching the Internet in the English language classroom*. Unpublished action research report, AMEP Research Centre, Sydney, Australia.

Todd, R. (2000). Negotiating the Web: Language, critical literacies and learning. In D. Gibbs & K. Krause (Eds.), *Cyberlines*. Melbourne: James Nicholas Publishers.

Thurston, J. (2003). *Webpages: Advice for teachers*. Unpublished report, AMEP Research Centre, Sydney, Australia.

## Chapter 2

Ho Mei Lin, C. (1997). Teachers' tips: Online grammar teaching and learning. *The Internet TESL Journal*, III(12).

Jones, G. (2000). *How do I learn to speak? A review of the possibilities and constraints of online language learning*. London: London University Institute of Education.

King Koi, N. (2002). *Using the Internet in the AMEP classroom with multi-level classes*. Unpublished action research report, AMEP Research Centre, Sydney, Australia.

Kung, S.-C., & Chuo, T.-W. (2002). Students' perceptions of English learning through ESL/EFL websites. *TESL-EJ*, 6(1).

Mello, V. (1997). Online quizzes – are they worthwhile? *The Internet TESL Journal*, VIII(7).

Moote, S. (2002). Evaluation considerations for on-line ESL courses. *The Internet TESL Journal*, VIII(3).

Schrock, K. (1998). Separating the wheat from the chaff: How to tell the good sites from the bad. Retrieved July 19, 2002, from Kathy Schrock's guide for educators, from http://school.discovery.com/schrockguide/chaff.html

Soltesz, S. (1996). Writing World Wide Web pages as an educational tool. *CAELL Journal*, 7(1/2), 3–6.

Unat, H. (2002). *How to utilise ESL websites in the classroom*. Unpublished action research report, AMEP Research Centre, Sydney, Australia.

## Chapter 3

Blatnik, B. (2002). *ESL listening resources on the Web*. Unpublished action research report, AMEP Research Centre, Sydney, Australia.

Brown, G. (1977). *Listening to spoken English* (2nd ed.). Applied Linguistics and Language Study Series. C. Candlin (Ed.). London: Longman.

Buck, G. (1999). The testing of listening in a second language. In C. D. C. Chaplin (Ed.), *Encyclopaedia of language and education*. (Vol. 7. Language Testing and Assessment, pp. 64–74). Netherlands: Klower Academic Publishers.

Burns, A. H. J. (1997). *Focus on speaking*. Sydney: NCELTR.

Chaudron, C., Loschky, L., & Cook, J. (1994). Second language listening comprehension and lecture note-taking. In J. Flowerdew (Ed.), *Academic listening: Research perspectives*. Cambridge: University Press.

Cziko, G., & Park, S. (2003). Internet audio communication for second language learning: A comparative review of six programs. *Language Learning and Technology*, 7(1), 15–27.

Hoven, D. (1999). A model for listening and viewing comprehension in multimedia environments. *Language Learning and Technology*, 3(1), 88–103.

Nunan, D. (1997). Approaches to teaching listening in the language classroom. Proceedings of *Korea TESOL Conference*, (pp. 1–10).

Nunan, D., & Miller, L. (Eds.). (1995). *New ways in teaching listening*. Alexandria: TESOL.

Peterson, M. (2001). Listening websites on the World Wide Web. *TESL EJ*, 5(1).

Rost, M. (1994). *Introducing listening*. London: Penguin English.

Rost, M. (2002). *Teaching and researching listening*. Harlow: Pearson Education.

Ur, P. (1984). (Ed.). *Teaching listening comprehension*. New York, NY: Cambridge University Press.

## Chapter 4

Endres, S. (2002). *Web publishing and ESL*. Unpublished action research report, AMEP Research Centre, Sydney, Australia.

Glister, P. (1997). *Digital literacy*. New York: John Wiley & Sons.

Hoven, D. (in press). Communicating and interacting: An exploration of the changing roles of media. *CALICO Journal*.

Kalyuga, S. (2000). When using sound with a text or picture is not beneficial for learning. *Australian Journal of Educational Technology*, 16(1), 161–172.

King Koi, N. (2002). *Using the Internet in the AMEP classroom with multi-level classes*. Unpublished research report, AMEP Research Centre, Sydney, Australia.

Lipscomb, P. (2002). *Reading what? on the Web*. Unpublished action research report, AMEP Research Centre, Sydney, Australia.

Mansfield, S. (2002). *Taming and teaching the Internet in the English language classroom*. Unpublished action research report, AMEP Research Centre, Sydney, Australia.

Nielsen, J. (1998). Conservatism of Web users. Retrieved May 5, 2004, from http://www.useit.com/alertbox/980322.html

Ramm, J. (1995). *Signposts*. Melbourne: AMES Victoria.

Snyder, I. (2002). *Silicon literacies*. London: Routledge.

Whitbred, D. (2001). *The design manual*. Sydney: UNSW Press.

## Chapter 5

Brinton, D. M., Snow, M. A., & Wesche, M. B. (1989). *Content-based second language instruction*. New York: Newbury House.

Debski, R. (2005). *Project-oriented CALL*. Sydney, Australia: NCELTR.

Fried-Booth, D. L. (1997). *Project work* (8th ed.). Oxford: Oxford University Press.

King Koi, N. (2002). *Using the Internet in the AMEP classroom with multi-level classes*. Unpublished action research report, AMEP Research Centre, Sydney, Australia.

Lipscomb, P. (2002). *Reading what? on the Web*. Unpublished action research report, AMEP Research Centre, Sydney, Australia.

Mansfield, S. (2002). *Taming and teaching the Internet in the English language classroom*. Unpublished action research report, AMEP Research Centre, Sydney, Australia.

Moss, D., & Van Duzer, C. (1998). Project-based learning for adult English language learners. Retrieved September 13, 2002, from http://www.cal.org/ncle/digests/ProjBase.htm

Murray, D. E., & McPherson, P. (2004). *Navigating to read; reading to navigate*. Sydney, Australia: NCELTR.

Norton, P. (2002). *Using the Internet in the AMEP classroom*. Unpublished action research report, AMEP Research Centre, Sydney, Australia.

Tun, C. (2002). *Using the Internet to carry out job searches*. Unpublished action research report, AMEP Research Centre, Sydney, Australia.

Williams, A. (2004). *Fact sheet: Enhancing language teaching with content*. Sydney: AMEP Research Centre.

## Chapter 6

Al-Bataineh, A., Hamann, S., & Wiegel, L. (2000). Reflections on practice: Classroom observations. *ERIC database*.

Brown, I. (1999). Internet treasure hunts – a treasure of an activity for students learning English. *The Internet TESL Journal*, 5(3).

Burleson, O. C. (2001). Find a need and fill it: A WebQuest for life-long learners. Retrieved January, 2004, from http://www.lausd.k12.ca.us/lausd/offices/di/Burleson/Lessons/index.html

Dodge, B. (1995). WebQuests: A technique for Internet based learning. *Distance Educator*, 1(2), 10–13.

Dodge, B. (1997). Some thoughts about WebQuests. San Diego State University. Retrieved May 12, 2004, from http://webquest.sdsu.edu/about_webquests.html

Dutt-Doner, K. E. A. (2002). Actively engaging learners in interdisciplinary curriculum through the integration of technology. *Computers in the Schools*, 16(3/4), 151–166.

Emmert, P. (2003). Integrating WebQuests in ESL. Retrieved May 12, 2004, from http://www.call-esl.com/

Joyce, K., & Stohr-Hunt, P. (2004). Web-based projects. Retrieved May 12, 2004, from http://oncampus.richmond.edu/academics/education/projects/

March, T. (1998). Why WebQuests: An introduction. Retrieved February 22, 2005, from http://www.ozline.com/webquests/intro.html

Marco, M. J. L. (2002). Internet content-based activities for ESP. *English Teaching Forum*, 40(3). Retrieved May 12, 2004, from http://exchanges.state.gov/forum/vols/vol40/no3

Perrone, C., Clark, D., & Repenning, A. (1996). WebQuest: Substantiating education in edutainment through interactive learning games. *Computer Networks and ISDN Systems*, 28(7–11), 1307–1319.

Peterson, C., Caverley, D., & MacDonald, L. (2003). Techtalk: Developing academic literacy through Webquests. *Journal of Developmental Education*, 26(3), 38–39.

Starr, L. (2000). Meet Bernie Dodge – the Frank Lloyd Wright of learning environments. Retrieved May 17, 2004, from http://www.educationworld.com/a_tech/tech020.shtml

Starr, L. (2004). So you want to compete in the Olympics. Retrieved May 13, 2004, from http://www.educationworld.com/a_tech/webquest_orig/webquest_orig008b. shtml

## Chapter 7

Dabbagh, N. (2002). Using a Web-based course management tool to support face-to-face instruction. Retrieved March 13, 2002, from http://ts.mivu.org/default.asp?show=aarticle&id-938

Johnson. N. (2003). *Diminishing the distance*. Unpublished action research report, AMEP Research Centre, Sydney, Australia.

King Koi, N. (2002). *Using the Internet in the AMEP classroom with multi-level classes*. Unpublished action research report, AMEP Research Centre, Sydney, Australia.

McPherson, P., & Murray, D. E. (2003). *Communicating on the Net*. Sydney: NCELTR.

Palloff, R. M., & Pratt, K. (1999). *Building learning communities in cyberspace: Effective strategies for the online classroom*. San Francisco: Jossey-Bass.

Vazquez, M. A. (2002). *Integrating the Internet in language teaching: Personal and institutional factors*. Unpublished M.App.Ling. thesis, Macquarie University, Sydney, Australia.

## Chapter 8

Burch, R. O. (2001). Effective Web design and core communication issues: The missing components in Web based distance education. *Journal of Educational Multimedia and Hypermedia*, 10(4), 357–367.

Endres, S. (2002). *Web page publishing and ESL.* Unpublished action research report, AMEP Research Centre, Sydney, Australia.

Fox, G. (1998). The Internet: Making it work in the ESL classroom. *The Internet TESL Journal,* IV(9). Retrieved May 24, 2004, from http://iteslh.org

Kelly, C. (2000). Guidelines for designing a good website for ESL students. *The Internet TESL Journal,* VI(3). Retrieved May 24, 2004, from http://iteslh.org

King Koi, N. (2002). *Using the Internet in the AMEP classroom with multi-level classes.* Unpublished action research report, AMEP Research Centre, Sydney, Australia.

Nielsen, J., & Tahin, M. (2002). Building websites with depth. *New architect.* Retrieved January 14, 2004, from www.webtechniques.com/archives/2001/02nielsen/

Puetter, S. (2002). *Using the Internet in the classroom.* Unpublished action research report, AMEP Research Centre, Sydney, Australia.

Soltesz, S. (1996). Writing World Wide Web Pages as an educational tool. *CAELL Journal,* 7(1/2), 3–6.

**Note:** Unpublished AMEP Research Centre reports are available from the NCELTR Resource Centre, Macquarie University: http://www.nceltr.mq.edu.au/resources/